Dark Seduction and Persuasion Tactics

The Simplified Playbook of Charismatic Masters of Deception. Leveraging IQ, Influence, and Irresistible Charm in the Art of Covert Persuasion and Mind Games

Emory Green

CLAIM YOUR FREE GIFT

This book comes with a free bonus item.

Head straight to the last chapter to quickly claim your gift today!

TABLE OF CONTENTS

INTRODUCTION

What is seduction? There are so many different examples of it: the politician who draws crowds and followers who sometimes act like they're under a spell. The one who isn't conventionally attractive yet is constantly accompanied by beautiful partners. A speaker who holds the entire room enthralled. The woman you know with several kids who's always been able to find a man to take care of her. The man you and your friends talk about who seems to have a different lover every night of the week. Maybe you've been enticed by someone who's incredibly alluring, although you can't quite figure out why. Or you have friends who can't seem to resist these temptations in the flesh.

The power of seduction is undeniable. And yet, it doesn't seem entirely acceptable in a polite society. When the topic is discussed, it's morally ambiguous. Good? Bad? Somewhere in between? But seduction is a science and doesn't have to rely on opinions. The ability to fascinate others isn't just an art, but a science. Understanding human nature and psychology is key to learning seduction. Everyone can learn the tips and tricks, as long as they have a handle on the basics. Anyone reading this book can use the tools I describe to enchant and influence other people. Perhaps even more importantly, they can learn to recognize when someone is trying to seduce them, so whether you welcome the ploy or not, you'll understand what's going on.

Seduction comes with its own set of risks and rewards. The rewards from successfully seducing others can be incredibly gratifying! But there are risks, too. Be aware that there is a cost to playing this game. The book you're holding in your hands uncovers the secrets of both the advantages and the disadvantages of seduction. You'll understand what is going on behind the scenes of current seduction controversies, that is in addition to techniques you'll learn to attract others or to defend yourself. I'll also discuss the art and the science that drives this force inside us.

Let me be upfront: I'm not a "pick-up artist"! I'm a man of science who puts scientific findings into action. I've studied the research and I've also studied the powerful people - the "alphas" - who rule the world. These people run multi-million dollar companies and are looked up to by millions of people who want to know their secrets. One of their hidden advantages is the way they're able to wield the power of seduction. They're incredibly magnetic and people are strongly drawn to them. This is not an accident. It's the result of their knowledge of how to enchant people.

I wanted to spread this knowledge beyond these few alphas and make more of them if you are willing! Note that alphas are not exclusively male. There are plenty of women with this ability, too. The people with whom I've already shared this knowledge have been incredibly grateful for the experience. They've told me how many opportunities opened up for them once they began to implement these tools and how many opportunists they dodged once they understood what was going on! They've also been thankful for the blissful world that blossomed before them after I explained the techniques of seduction. No longer are they ignorant about the art and science behind the magic of the seducer. I'm excited that people are starting to realize how far they can go to achieve their dreams and desires once they start to use the information in this book.

I also realize as I spread this knowledge that it is helping people understand human nature so much better, once they understand that there is no magic spell, only the leverage of human desires. This is the kind of information people want to know, but no one wants to talk about it. By reading this book, you are setting the foundation for getting what you want.

Readers are often curious about how psychology and seduction work together. You might have read an article about the "art of seduction". But without the scientific background, it may sometimes seem TOO powerful and too potent of a force to be left in your untrained hands! Or maybe you have doubts about whether it works without any research behind it. This book shows you how potent a force seduction is, but one that relies on human nature and psychology, backed by data. Others who've absorbed this information found the power within themselves, understanding their nature and their ability to attract what they want from life and a partner.

Once you've read this book, you'll be in control of your power. You'll be more aware of your ability to entice others into doing as you would like them to do. Understanding the desires, strengths, and vulnerabilities of both your power and that of others will be yours. When you begin to use the techniques I describe in this book, you'll discover that you have an edge on success and happiness. More opportunities will begin to present themselves to you, not just in your career or in seeking romantic love, but in all aspects of your life.

Right now, successful people are using these tools. They're the ones with an edge. Do you want someone else to scoop up your dream life or your dream partner? They might not even know they're waiting for you. Someone else might be charming them while you're still trying to figure out what you want to do. Let's face it, there are plenty of others with this information who are treating you as prey because you don't have the tools yet. Become the seducer instead. Unlock the power in your nature to use it for good. As you'll discover later in this book, influencing others doesn't have to be predatory or manipulative. You can use it for the greater good, in addition to using it to your advantage.

Discover the secrets behind the art of seduction. Learn the science that underlies human nature and human psychology. Be empowered to choose your best life. This book doesn't judge you and your desires. At this point, the only person who can stop you from unlocking this power is you.

Enjoying this book so far? Remember to head to the bottom of this book for a bonus bite-sized yet valuable free resource on Conversational Hypnosis. This mini e-book is the easiest way to learn how to be a successful conversational hypnotist. Curious about the benefits it can do to your normal day to day conversations? Get your copy now! This free resource is available for a limited time only.

CHAPTER ONE:

True Seduction

What's the meaning of the word "seduction"? People often think of this power in relation to sex. A man who seduces women may be a "pick-up artist" or a Romeo. A woman who seduces men is a seductress (as is a woman who seduces other women). Think of the other ways in which you've heard the word "seduce" or "seduction". Some politicians are known for their charisma and their ability to make the person they're speaking with feel like the only one in the room. You may have heard popular or famous speakers "seduce" their audience with their magnetism. Excellent sales reps are sometimes also known to "seduce" their prospects into buying.

What do they all have in common?

Seduction: A simple definition

When looking at the dictionary, the ambiguous nature of the word is clear. Some of the meanings are negative, but others are positive.

1. To lead astray...corrupt.
2. To persuade or induce sexual intercourse.
3. To lead or draw away, as from principles...
4. To win over; attract; entice[1].

---

[1] https://www.dictionary.com/browse/seduce

.

Interestingly, the Latin root of the word is much more neutral. It comes from the Latin *"se ducere"*, which means "they lead". This is really what seduction is about: leading. Naturally, some leadership is bad, some is good, and some is neutral. You can think of seduction as leading someone. If you want the other person to have sex or fall in love with you, you're leading them to see you as an attractive person. When you're up on stage, you're leading the audience to listen to you and find you credible. If someone else is trying to seduce you, they're trying to lead you to what they want you to do.

The paradox of seduction

This type of power is inherently manipulative. However, seduction is not forceful. It's not rape, when looking at it in the context of love or sex. It's about the process and, more importantly, persuasion, not physical violence or threats. It's also not one-sided, so there is consent on both sides, at least at the end. It may not start this way. The seducer wants to get their way. When the other person succumbs, it's not because they've been forced to, either physically or mentally. They've succumbed because the seducer has made the prospect of conceding so alluring and so enticing. For example, consider a female virgin who's been enticed to have sex with a man for the first time. Because seduction is aimed at the sensual side of human nature and not the logical, rational side, she may very well come to view the encounter negatively. This could happen if she sees her capitulation to the seduction as being weak, or if she feels "used" and not cared for afterward.

On the other hand, someone who's been a virgin, possibly for longer than she would have liked, may feel liberated by having been "taken". A woman whose culture treats sex as dirty or wrong may subsequently feel relieved that she'd been taken. Or she may awaken to her own feminine power, which she may have been unaware of, or even told that she didn't possess.

"The desire of the man is for the woman, but the desire of the woman is for the desire of the man." - Madame de Stael

Seduction can wear many faces, so it's too simplistic to suggest that the results are always negative for the one seduced. Seduction can be pleasurable and also paradoxical: the effects may be positive and/or negative. The truth is that many people want to be seduced. They want to feel special, to fall under a spell, if even for a short time, and to be appreciated and be viewed as worthy of seduction. When it comes to sex, arousal is one of the most potent human experiences - most of us want more of it! The thrill of seduction is the anticipation of it. Not the culmination of desire, or the achievement of the goal. The excitement comes in savoring the process and stretching out the length of the game in order to fully enjoy it. Anticipation is key to the enjoyment of many experiences - even vacations. The pleasure of thinking about an upcoming vacation can sometimes even outweigh the happiness you feel on the trip itself![2] Many people find a happier life when they spend more time enjoying the lead-up to big, fun events and slow down and savor the moment.

The difference between seduction, persuasion, and manipulation

These three ways of communicating in order to influence other people are closely linked, but they don't all mean the same thing. The word with a more positive connotation is "persuasion", which is simply communication intended to alter another person's behavior. There's no stress on the person being persuaded and they are aware of the intent. No one is hiding anything and the facts are known to both sides. Persuaders often use logical arguments to make their case. The other person is free to question the assumptions. If they find the argument holds, they may

---

[2] https://www.psychologytoday.com/us/blog/shameless-woman/201207/the-power-seduction

7

well accept the case that's made and change their behavior, as the persuader hoped.

Ads often use well-known techniques to persuade their audience to purchase something. Emotional appeal, the bandwagon effect, and other methods are common. Design and color are also used to create campaigns that will bring in buyers. Although some of these approaches are known to and understood by the wider audience, some of them are not. This brings us into the other two above-mentioned arenas, where both sides are not equally equipped to handle the attempted influence.

While manipulation is intentional, just as persuasion is, part of this intent is to deceive the one being manipulated. Facts or knowledge is hidden in order to bring about the results that the manipulator wants. You might sometimes see this in person, but it's also common in marketing and political campaigns, where the manipulator tries to give only a little to receive a lot. One well-known manipulative device is reciprocity[3], in which the one doing the manipulating gives a little something which makes the receiver feel obligated to do what they want.

A political campaign might send out buttons or stickers, so the receivers feel obligated to donate to the campaign and perhaps volunteer on the ground. Many nonprofit groups send out all kinds of items - bags, calendars, umbrellas, and t-shirts - to get donations. They're relying on a characteristic of human nature which tells us that if someone gives you something, whether or not you asked for it, you're obliged to reciprocate.

Sellers often manipulate buyers. They assess the buyer's purchasing power and then use one technique or another to sell something more expensive. Ever feel manipulated in a car dealership? There's a reason for that! Manipulation is temporary because the person being manipulated will no longer trust the other. Relationships are based on trust and communication. Once that's breached, the two sides cannot maintain a relationship. Persuasion and seduction are normally longer

---

[3] http://opinionsandperspectives.blogspot.com/2010/11/persuasion-manipulation-seduction-and.html

processes because manipulation works only over a short period of time. Unlike the logical use of persuasion, manipulation is based on emotions.

Seduction lies somewhere between manipulation and persuasion. Like manipulation, the seducer plays on their target's emotions. They're not as open as if they were simply trying to persuade the other to do something. They may hide their true intentions. For example, a Romeo may entice a woman into believing that a romantic relationship is on offer, when really they just want to have sex. But the deceit is more subtle and less coercive than with manipulation. There's a promise made to the other, just as in persuasion - but the promise is more likely to go unfulfilled in a seduction.

Ads and movies are particularly susceptible to making empty promises. How often have you seen an ad for a food that made you so hungry you had to buy it, only to realize that the product looks nothing like what was shown on TV (this is especially true for fast-food restaurants) and it didn't even taste very good. Or maybe you saw a trailer for a movie that looked terrific, but the movie itself was only ho-hum? These ads and trailers were seductive, not truthful.

Modern seduction techniques

Successful businesses focus on pleasing the customer. Companies known for terrific customer service, or excellent conversion turning them into clients, have always been able to create the idea of an ideal world - one where there are fewer problems, less pain, and more pleasure. Humans tend to be averse to loss, so the avoidance of pain actually is more important than the creation of more pleasure. Humans also tend to be attracted to uncertainty. A man who makes his attraction obvious to a woman is less desirable than a man who sends conflicting signals. In turn, men are enticed by a "coquette": a woman who teases, flirts, and denies.[4] This type of seduction stands out in a world where people are

---

[4] https://coolcommunicator.com/social-seduction-creating-space-anticipation/

often aggressive when trying to sell you on what they want. This "scarcity effect" also provides good results for marketers. "Act now or the bonus will be gone" will often prod customers into action. As mass media and advertising work together to seduce consumers into spending their money, it's important to remember that consumers respond to these messages. We are all contributing to the society in which we live, not just as consumers, but also as human beings searching for romantic partners.

Now that women have their own ways of making a living, they're not as dependent on men as they were generations ago. Men have to provide an emotional reason for a woman to go out with and have sex with them. They need to seduce in a way that might not have been necessary centuries ago. For a long time, it was assumed that women only "put up" with sex. This may have had something to do with the fact that she had to marry quickly if she wanted to be taken care of. We, in the modern world, know that women like sex, but they can't be seen to enjoy it too much, lest they are called a slut, or worse. Women want to be seduced and romanced and feel attractive and alluring. Teasing, flirting, and seducing a woman are all modern ways for a man to have the relationship he wants. Drawing out the anticipation for both of them makes it even more pleasurable. The key here is that logic has nothing to do with it! It's all about playing with emotional appeal and it's a social game, not a rational one.

Chapter Summary

- Seduction comes from the Latin "they lead" and, depending on the context, may be seen as positive or negative. Sometimes both.
- People want to be seduced, whether it's by a potential lover or something else.
- Seduction as an influencing technique is less open and more emotional than persuasion, yet less deceitful than manipulation.

- Modern seduction techniques recognize that we know more about human nature than ever before.
- Since women can live independently in a way they couldn't before, men seeking a woman need to use seductive techniques if they want a romantic/sexual relationship with a woman.

In the next chapter, you will learn about the history and psychological background of sexual seducers, including famous ones.

CHAPTER TWO:

The Names and Faces of Seduction

When talking about romantic and sexual seduction, there are plenty who have gone before us. Men and women throughout the ages have understood how to use human nature to influence others to get what they want. There are different types of seducers and they have similar traits. You'll probably find it helpful to learn from those who have mastered the techniques of seduction.

Famous seducers in history

You've probably heard of Giacomo Casanova since many male seducers are commonly called "Casanovas". He was a Venetian who loved to love ladies in trouble. He'd solve her problem and give her little gifts before enticing her into his bed. Then, he'd get bored and leave. Sounds familiar, right? Notice how he started the seduction, though, once he selected his target: he got her out of whatever difficulty she was in. In other words, he was the "white knight" who came to her rescue.

Another well-known male seducer was the Englishman, Lord Byron. A poet and a soldier, he was a man of action who could write and he was catnip to the ladies (and to men as well). The movie star Errol Flynn swashed and buckled with the best of them. Even accusations of statutory rape didn't hurt his reputation, though that might be different if he were swashing today.

Famous basketball player Wilt Chamberlain claimed to have slept with over 20,000 women. The numbers seem mathematically suspicious; given that he would have had to have eight different women every week after he turned 16. The women he hit on noticed that, although he was confident in himself (being a 7-foot-tall rich man probably didn't hurt), he was still respectful of them. More recently, Jack Nicholson and Russell Brand, both performers, are known to have mastered the techniques of seduction. Nicholson is famous for his bad-boy attitude and the up-to-no-good gleam in his eye. Brand is better known for his wit and charm…plus his hair!

The club to which famous seducers belong is by no means a male-only institution. Cleopatra, the last Pharaoh of Egypt, played the coquette. She used both Mark Antony and Julius Caesar to work her "magic". Catherine the Great of Russia used her affairs differently. After she tired of her lovers, she gave them good jobs in her government. And in the case of former lover Potemkin, they helped her procure new lovers that met her standards for intelligence, as well as performance in bed.

The rise of seduction communities

In the game of seduction, when thinking about men seducing women, men have always needed to stand out in the crowd and make the woman feel special, then to win her trust and ultimately a place in her bed. Many men might dream about leaping from standing out in the crowd to going to bed, without all that work in the middle.

In Scotland in the 1600s, it was believed there was a secret word a man could whisper in a woman's ear to get her into bed without all the work of winning her over. This word was protected by a secret order of men who trained horses. The society, known as the "Horseman's Word", also guarded agrarian rituals that involved the magical word, thought to have been provided by Old Scratch himself.[5] The word caused horses to

---

[5] https://www.ancient-origins.net/history/enchanted-sex-word-scotland-s-secret-seduction-society-008114

halt until the horseman released them from their spell and it also rendered women powerless against a seducer. In fact, unmarried girls who were impregnated by horsemen weren't looked down upon, because the devil's power in the word made them helpless. In other words, it wasn't her fault that the word had been used against her.

The society was like a trade union protecting horsemen. The best of these horse trainers were granted special benefits: the word that dominated horses and women and higher pay. It also behaved like the Masons, with secret handshakes and the like. Once landowners used tractors instead of horses, the Horseman's Word was absorbed into Masonic temples. It turns out, at least according to more modern members of the society, that the power didn't come so much from a word as it did a potent blend of oils and herbs that attracted both women and horses.

In the 20th and 21st centuries, seducers began to form communities, particularly through the internet. In the early days, young men mostly had to rely on their peers (who generally knew as little as they did) or, if they were lucky, older male mentors for information about dating and finding a desirable woman. More information became available with the rise of magazines like Playboy, which advertised books such as the 1970s classic "How to Pick Up Women" by Eric Weber.[6] This may be where the term "pick-up artist" originated.

However, when the AIDS crisis hit in the 1980s, advice veered back toward staying safe during sex. The 1990s and Oprah brought women's sexual needs into the mainstream. By the turn of the century, with the rise of the internet, communities for men to learn the art of seduction began to flourish. From the mysteries of neurolinguistic programming (NLP), which is essentially the same as hypnosis, to "negging", men taught other men about more modern, or at least updated techniques. To neg a woman is to give her a backhanded compliment, like telling her she's "cute - like my bratty little sister."[7] This method was intended for

---

[6] https://historycooperative.org/the-history-of-the-seduction-community/
[7] https://historycooperative.org/the-history-of-the-seduction-community/

use on beautiful, glamorous, and secure women, to pique their interest instead of fawning over them as so many men did. Unfortunately, in the wrong hands, the technique could develop backlash. Men used it on insecure women or those who weren't conventionally attractive, causing heartache and damage, instead of the space for the game of seduction.

Internet message boards became a place for men to congregate anonymously and share their seduction theories. They were able to share stories of what worked and what didn't, from a strictly male point of view and without worrying about family values. One of these men was known as "Mystery", famous for wearing a top hat and a feather boa. He referred to this as "peacocking", or spreading a magnificent display to attract a female of the species. He also did magic tricks to entice young women. Young men imitated him in his "pick-up artist" image. So many men were members of "The Community" online, that eventually, a man named Neil Strauss wrote a book on the movement, entitled, "The Game: Penetrating the Secret Society of Pick-Up Artists". The book and a TV show on VH1 made pick up artistry even more popular, to the point that most young men had heard of it. Some dismissed it, but others studied it closely to find the secrets of seducing women.

Feeding on its popularity, men who called themselves gurus of the game could just walk in off the street and claim to be experts. Books, CDs, seminars, and boot camps flooded the market. Groups of men began to go out and hit on women to try out the techniques. To beat the competition, some in the community began to focus on the psychology of the game and how young men were getting in their own way due to inner hang-ups and roadblocks. Currently, the community is concerned more about physical and mental fitness in order to make themselves an alluring target for women, rather than trying to hit up women in packs.

There are now plenty of communities on the internet that provide dating advice. They seem to be less concentrated on gurus and what experts have to say and more about crowdsourcing advice. Tactics in many cases are more about seduction and less about outright manipulation, which is a trap that pick-up artists often fall into.

The Dark Triad of seducers

As mentioned in the introduction, there is a science behind the art of seduction. In the examples above, men have relied mostly on the art. Gossip, what was passed down from other men, the examples other seducers set, and the like. Science has identified three psychological traits that are often found in successful seducers, known as the Dark Triad. The three are narcissism, psychopathy, and Machiavellianism.

What exactly are these traits? Narcissism is demonstrated by dominance, a grandiose view of oneself, and a sense of entitlement. It's been shown that this trait is primarily male and it exists in all kinds of cultures.[8] A narcissist finds it easy to lure someone into bed and then kick them out a short time after sex. It works well for casual sex, which has greater negative consequences for women (pregnancy, slut-shaming), so men are also more likely to be interested in casual sex than women. Since narcissists tend to parade their resources more than other men, they are sometimes more attractive to women.

Men also tend to score higher on having Machiavellian impulses than women do. This trait involves being deceitful, manipulative, and insincere. They're known to pretend to be in love to get the casual sex they want - this trait is also conducive to casual sex, as is psychopathy, where people are callous, lack empathy, and can be hostile to others. Overlaid with this is a superficial charm and people with this characteristic tend to have many sexual partners and also be rated more attractive, not only by themselves, but also by women. Yet again, this trait is more common in men than it is in women. The Dark Triad appears to favor what the scientists call "short-term mating". The rest of us refer to this as casual sex. The question then is, why do women go for men with the Dark Triad or even one of these personality characteristics? Evolutionary psychological theory claims that women, who must be more sexually selective than men due to the higher cost of sex for them,

---

[8] https://scottbarrykaufman.com/wp-content/uploads/2013/09/The-Dark-Triad-Personality.pdf

have certain traits they look for in a man. It's to their benefit to choose a dominant man because these men can typically obtain more resources for the family. Dominant men are usually confident and assertive. Dark Triad attributes create the illusion for women that the man is socially dominant, whether or not he actually is. A man who's anti-social appears strong and masculine, a psychopath appears to be confident, and aggressive men tend to come off as dominant. A man with a grandiose sense of himself comes off as ambitious and driven, which are also features of dominant men. Someone who's high on the Machiavellian scale tends to accumulate power and understands it almost intuitively, which may suggest to the female observer that he himself is powerful.

Earlier, I talked about leaving some uncertainty as catnip for a potential sexual partner. Men who rate high in Dark Triad traits tend not to care what others think of them, which is a technique that stands out to people-pleasers. That little frisson of danger makes the game of seduction all the more exciting for the one being seduced.

Can you think of anyone you know who's a great example of the Dark Triad? I'll give you one: James Bond. He's always seducing a new lover and he doesn't stick around afterward. The women in the movie fall for it every time, but this is not so far from real life!

Narcissism has been shown to rate higher in dating than the other features of the Triad.[9] The charm and attentiveness that goes along with this trait tends to be more attractive to women, compared to Machiavellianism or psychopathy. These characteristics can help men get ahead at work, not just in the mating game. The characteristics of the Dark Triad are also linked with openness to new experience, high self-esteem, and curiosity, which are also attractive features in the boardroom. In addition, the Triad tends to enhance competitiveness. Ranking high in characteristics surrounding psychopathy and

---

[9] https://www.sciencedirect.com/science/article/abs/pii/S0191886913006582

Machiavellianism frightens off would-be competitors and is attractive to superiors.[10]

However, although these behaviors are to an individual's advantage, it causes harm to the organization. Dark Triad employees freeride on other employee's coattails. They're more likely to steal from the company, sabotage it, and not bother to show up when they don't feel like it. Although they may have personal success, their actual work performance is poor. The superiors they have seduced along the way ignore their lack of productivity.

If you're not psychotic about it, some aspects of Dark Triad attributes can actually be used for the greater good. Leaders have to make unpopular decisions, so it's best if you're a leader not to care too much about what other people think. Special Forces and other elite squads have to move on from pulling the trigger and killing someone else, lest they are killed themselves. Surgeons have to emotionally detach from the fact that they're cutting into another person's body in order to perform it successfully. Moderate Dark Triad traits can also benefit an organization. Those who are intermediate in Machiavellianism are often good employees because they're good with networking and managing. Military leaders who can key in on the bright side of narcissism with egoism and high self-esteem, but moderate their manipulativeness, are often very effective. In other words, lower doses of Dark Triad attributes can be beneficial! Too much and we see the dark side of them.

Alpha males and alpha females

Where did the concept of "alpha males" come from in the first place? The origin of this term comes from animal studies, where an alpha male is literally the leader of the pack. Alphas in these types of hierarchical animal groups are high-status and have access to more resources than other males. Typically, determining which member of an animal group

---

[10] https://hbr.org/2015/11/why-bad-guys-win-at-work

is the alpha can be made by observing the males as they fight each other. The winner becomes the alpha and gets to choose whichever mate he wants. He is in a position of power.

Human males in a position of power are known to exploit women for their benefit. They do it because they can and they're in a position to do so. However, not all alphas are men. Some are women. They're talented, ambitious, and driven. An alpha female is confident and believes (like her male counterparts) that her potential for achievement has no limits. They're able to regulate their emotions because they have EQ or emotional intelligence. This allows them to smooth over social and business interactions. As part of their EQ, they can set the tone for other women to have good discussions without falling prey to backbiting and gossip. They have a deep drive to learn more and become experts in their chosen subjects. Known for both their mental and physical strength, an alpha female is not only asked for help, but is comfortable asking for help when she needs it. She tends to come from solid family foundations, which makes it easier for her to venture out into new experiences. There can be only one alpha female, but for an organization to run well, there should be one (instead of none).

However, men can't be divided into alphas and betas, as pop culture and earlier alpha male studies would have it! In the absence of context, women don't find domineering men or submissive men attractive, which suggests that there's more than one way to attract women.[11] When dominance becomes aggressive, it's a turnoff. But when dominant means confident and assertive, women are attracted. Women don't mind so much if dominant men want to compete with each other, but they don't find men who might become aggressive with them a turn-on. In fact, women like dominant men best when they are agreeable and not narcissistic.

In humans, it's not always about physical strength. Men can become sexually desirable when they acquire prestige, which can come through

---

[11] https://greatergood.berkeley.edu/article/item/the_myth_of_the_alpha_male

social channels. Actual performance is a factor in genuine self-esteem, which is an attractive characteristic. Being alpha is also context-specific: a CEO of a large multinational corporation will no longer be the alpha in the general population of a prison.

While dominance may be desirable in a harsh or extreme environment, prestige provides men with more resources in more situations, which is more attractive than someone who uses coercion and force in "polite" society. An alpha with prestige is not only considered stronger, but also more moral and socially skilled. An alpha who is "merely" dominant may be rated as strong, but not thought of as ethical or skilled.[12]

The nine types of seducers

Now that you have a background in the psychology and history of seducers, both male and female, you may want to understand the different ways in which seducers operate. Maybe one of them will resonate with you. Or, maybe you'll understand the seducer in your life a little bit better.

Rake

This seducer is driven by his libido. Women are charmed by his intense desire. They don't get defensive around him because he doesn't seem to be holding anything back. The Rake's attention and passion seem all-consuming. Many women ignore the red flags because he doesn't come across as calculating. Words are his weapon. Women find men good at wordplay alluring, and the Rake milks it for all he's worth when he's in pursuit. He won't stick around for very long and marriage is definitely not what he sees in the cards for himself. Lord Byron and Errol Flynn were both Rakes.

---

[12] https://greatergood.berkeley.edu/article/item/the_myth_of_the_alpha_male

Ideal Lover

An Ideal Lover may be male or female. Either way, they reflect the fantasy of whoever they're trying to seduce. Casanova became the white knight that the women he chased wanted. He'd study a woman as he pursued her, discovering what it was she wanted, and then gave it to her, unless, of course, she wanted marriage.

Madame de Pompadour started in life as a middle-class woman, but she seduced King Louis XV of France by being what he wanted in a mistress. She never allowed him to be bored, which was exactly what he wanted.

Interestingly, being an Ideal Lover doesn't just work in romance: politicians benefit when they mirror what the electorate wants, as in the case of President John F. Kennedy.

Dandy

Many of us feel it necessary to obey gender roles - masculine and short-haired for men, feminine with long hair for women. We tend to be intrigued with those that are more fluid, or who present differently from their gender. A feminine Dandy is a man who often pays more attention to his clothes, hair, and figure than most men do, but still has something about him that seems dangerous - this is very enticing for women!

Rudolph Valentino dressed in flowing robes and wore a lot of makeup for his role in the movie "The Sheik", yet since he still came off with a little danger, women loved him. Being a Dandy is not just being effeminate because, without a touch of menace, this isn't seductive to women. Similarly, a masculine Dandy creates excitement and confusion for her potential lovers. George Sand was a well-known woman who wore men's clothing in an exaggerated way.

Whether male or female, the Dandy is all about the pleasure of living, including eating wonderful food and living with beautiful objects.

Charmer

To be a Charmer, all you need to do is deflect attention away from yourself and onto your target. Make the person you're with feel better about themselves because you don't argue or hassle them. The more you do so, the more power you have over them. Unfortunately for some of you, this type is the seducer without sex! There's always sexual tension, but it goes unresolved. Charmers flatter the self-esteem and vanity of others. If there's any unpleasantness, the Charmer remains unruffled.

Catherine the Great, arriving in Russia as a young German princess, bided her time. She charmed the court by acting as if she had no interest in power at all. Pamela Churchill (who was married to Winston Churchill's son at the time) wooed the wealthy widower Averell Harriman. Though at first, the hostesses in Washington D.C. were suspicious of her, she charmed them, too. She later became a noted hostess and philanthropist.

Benjamin Disraeli charmed Queen Victoria when he was Prime Minister. He sent her copies of reports and made other concessions to her. In response, she made him an earl. He understood that her sober exterior hid the heart of a woman who wanted some seduction in her life.

Charmers seduce by not talking much about themselves. They know where to focus: on their target, and they do so subtly. It's not the harsh, glaring light of attention but more of a pleasant glow that makes the other person feel warm and special.

Charismatic

This seducer has an inner quality that creates an intense presence. It's often an intense self-confidence, but might also be boldness or an inner serenity. They leave the source of it a mystery, but people are drawn to the way the quality displays itself. They're leaders, often mass leaders, and their targets want to be led. Charismatics play with repressed sexuality, but their appeal is actually quasi-religious. Their victims see their extraordinary quality, whatever it is, as a sign from God. How else could they have it and be so different from everyone else?

A Charismatic tends to be theatrical and play with language. They don't seem entirely safe, but call for adventure and excitement. Joan of Arc's intense visions made her a Charismatic. Rasputin seduced early-1900s Russia, particularly Tsar Alexander and his wife the Tsarina. He never tried to downplay his contradictions, which the (highly artificial) court found entirely alluring. Elvis Presley had some demons and when they came out in his music, they exhibited a sexual power. He had a stutter that only went away when he performed.

A good example of a political Charismatic was the Russian Communist, Lenin. He was not only incredibly confident, but determined and organized in his work. He excited workers into revolution. The Argentine radio star Eva Duarte married Juan Peron, who was then elected President. Though she went from soap operas to more serious speeches, she touched everyone who listened to her. Another Charismatic who was a master of language was Malcolm X. He helped a long-oppressed portion of society release their emotions with his speeches and actions.

Being a successful Charismatic depends on being successful. Once the audience believes that you're losing, they'll turn against you.

Natural

Some people are easily seduced by a lover with the playfulness of a child. Adulthood can be extremely artificial, never saying what you want to say to your boss or friends. Naturalness in an adult is enticing. A Natural seducer retains the spirit of childhood, but when calculating who and how to seduce, they're very adult.

Charlie Chaplin found that he was alluring to any number of women by playing up his weakness. He made people at once feel sympathy for him and also superior to him, which is an incredibly seductive place to be. Josephine Baker took Paris by storm. She refused to be loyal to any club, creating space for the managers to chase her. Because she played her roles so lightly, the Parisians never tired of her.

Star

Although our lives are no longer nasty, brutish, and short, they can still be quite harsh! The Star makes people want to watch them, though no one is allowed up close. They allow us to use our imaginations for what a fantastic life they must lead, while keeping their distance at the same time.

JFK kept America guessing what was behind his eyes and smile. His effect was deliberate, not accidental. Marlene Dietrich was famous for the coldness which overlay her beauty and her face was a blank mask onto which directors could project anything they wanted.

A Star appears like a myth or dream come to life. They avoid direct answers and appearing too real. They allow their fans to know something about them, which paradoxically makes them want to know more. But a true Star doesn't let anyone know everything about them because part of their allure is the fantasy that others project onto them.

Siren

This type is normally a woman - a siren is a seductress. She takes her name from the goddesses whose song was so sweet they caused sailors to crash upon rocky shores. She's a woman who loves sex and uses it to get what she wants.

Cleopatra is a famous example of this type. Sirens provide theatrics and drama that enthrall men. They embody a man's fantasy and there's no need to be conventionally attractive to put a man under a Siren's spell. Marilyn Monroe is another example. She taught herself how to be more enticing to men and she was successful. Her breathy voice made them want to get closer to her to listen. Her touch of vulnerability, which for her was a need for affection, drew men to her.

A siren offers a little bit of danger with her pleasure, which is extremely alluring.

Coquette

This seducer is the master (or mistress) of teasing - of promising yet never delivering total satisfaction. They make their lovers wait until they're ready and delay satisfaction as long as they like.

"...[W]e are only really excited by what is denied us, by what we cannot possess in full." - Robert Greene

Josephine alternately coaxed Napoleon Bonaparte to her and sent him away without seeing him, which both enraged and excited him. Warhol became famous when he stopped begging for people to notice him and instead withdrew from others. Coquettes are not jealous themselves, but incite jealousy by paying attention to a third party, which drives their intended target wild with desire. It's incredibly effective on a group as well, as dictators Mao Zedong and Josef Tito demonstrated.

To seduce, you have to have some measure of self-esteem and self-confidence. If you're insecure and too vulnerable, it's a turn-off. There's a bit of sexual tension underlying every type of seduction, more pronounced in some and less in others. Being able to entice another human being means observing them closely enough to play on others' emotions and weaknesses.

Chapter Summary

- There have been all kinds of seducers throughout history and studying how they were able to attract others can help those who seek to become seducers themselves.
- Seduction communities come and go with the zeitgeist and currently focus on the seducer becoming more appealing to their potential lovers.

- The Dark Triad of seduction includes narcissism, Machiavellianism, and psychopathy. Moderate expressions of these traits are more beneficial than strong expressions.
- Though we commonly discuss alpha males, there are alpha females as well, though their characteristics are often different from their male counterparts.
- Anyone looking to improve their seduction game can examine the nine archetypes of seducers and take their cues from them.

In the next chapter, we'll discuss the elements necessary for successful seduction.

CHAPTER THREE:

Elements of Seduction

Let's break down the art of seduction a little more. You probably aren't enthralled by every person you meet because not everyone has that certain something that's necessary to be alluring. If you are enthralled by every person you meet, that's a different matter! When you're easily seduced, people have more power over you than they should. Recognizing what a Rake is doing, for example, will help you avoid being so quickly placed under another person's spell.

What do seducers have that others don't?

We can actually define that "certain something". There is a range of behaviors seen in the various types of seducers, as we discussed in chapter two, however, they do tend to have some qualities in common. Because people tend to be attracted to those who are confident and personable, a seducer will at least appear to have these attributes too, otherwise, their ploys can't get off the ground! They're charismatic and passionate, believing very deeply in themselves and also in being positive. No matter what happens, they are not easily ruffled or thrown off their game.

You know by now that one of the quirks of human nature is that we like a bit of a challenge and prefer that the prize is not given up too fast. Someone who is at least a little bit distant, or alternately repels and coaxes us toward them, is highly desirable. Seducers maintain this aura of mystery. We find elusiveness intriguing. Interested? Not interested? People keep coming back for more. These seducers also may appear to be in tune with their targets. They seem to be more sensitive to others' needs, sometimes presenting the solution before their audience has even mentioned the problem! They want to get to know their target, in order to push the right buttons. The target feels special because the seducer is investing so much time and attention in them. The seducer may also reveal their carefully chosen vulnerabilities, knowing that their target will feel it necessary to respond in kind.

Knowing that people enjoy being led, a seducer's voice is always calm and controlled. They like wordplay, especially of the suggestive kind! They're also in control of their body movements. Their gestures may not be easy to read or overt since they're carefully cultivating that air of ambiguity that human beings are so intrigued by. They will make a lot of eye contact, being very attentive when they're drawing in their targets.

Who is easily seduced?

When it comes to romantic entanglement, there are women with certain qualities and in situations who are more prone to being seduced, which ends in heartbreak for them when the seducer gets bored and takes off, as they inevitably do. If you resonate with any of these characteristics, be wary when someone magnetic and charming crosses your path!

Constantly dissatisfied

Someone who is always complaining and sad is easily swept off their feet. Seducers temporarily lift the sadness, as they act interested in the complainer and make them feel special. They're also great at concocting a fantasy of a better and more romantic world, compared to the reality of life.

If this is you, there are a number of ways to either change your reality or change the way you look at it. The first is to have an attitude of gratitude. What can you be grateful for in your life? What do you love about your life? Reality can't be all rainbows and puppies all the time, unfortunately. But the more you find things to like about your life and change the things you don't like, the less you'll need a fantasy. The seducer will be less attractive to you, simply because they can't really offer you anything that you want.

Active imagination

Seducers give off signals. Their actions wave red flags for those who are paying attention. But a target with an imagination doesn't see the obvious signs that they're dealing with a seducer who is planning to love them and leave them. Seducers induce fantasies that can be easily pictured by someone with a good imagination. The target can get so wound up in the beautiful future that the seducer promises that they miss the cues which would otherwise tell them that it is not going to happen. They're also very skilled with language and it's easy to be caught up in their words.

Make sure, if you know you possess a vivid imagination, that you are looking at your potential lover's actions, not just listening to their fantasies. That will help you see the red flags when they begin waving.

You typically ignore red flags and the opinions of family and friends

Similar to those with active imaginations, you're so immersed in the fantasy and the charm that you ignore the signs you should be heeding. You have arguments which suggest that you're incompatible because you don't share common values, or the other person doesn't seem to ever want to do what you want to do. Your friends and/or family warn you about the signs they see. Perhaps they know people who've been burned by your seducer, they've seen them around town in the company of attractive people, or they can see that the seducer is making you unhappy.

Or maybe your behavior has changed for the worse. They love you and want the best for you.

It's true that sometimes other people won't be able to see what you see in someone and that's not always a bad thing. But if everyone around you is telling you the same thing, you should listen to what they have to say.

People-pleaser

The reality is that many people, women especially, are socialized to please others. They go through life believing that their value and worthiness depends on external approval. It's not entirely surprising that people-pleasers fall under a charming spell so easily. When the seducer pulls back, as they must, the people-pleaser will do anything to win back that approval and attention. Otherwise, they'll end up feeling worthless or that they're not good enough to be loved.

If this is you, working on your need for external approval will help you immensely, and not just to repel or ignore seducers! You are worthy of love, no matter what anyone says, and you need to love yourself first. Only once you've achieved this should you search for a romantic partner. Kick 'em to the curb if they start withdrawing and find another one!

Willing to use sex to try for love

Someone with low self-esteem is often willing to have sex too soon, in the hopes that it will lead to love. But with a seducer, it only leads to a broken heart because they are only in it for the sex.

Oxytocin is a neurochemical that promotes bonding and women release it when they have sex. They may end up feeling bonded to the man they just had sex with, who could not be feeling less willing to partner up with them! If this is you, be choosier about who you have sex with. Ask yourself what will happen if you have sex with a certain person and it doesn't become love. If you don't like the consequences, avoid going to bed with them.

You make bad compromises for the sake of the relationship

New people in your life bring new adventures and that's not a bad thing! When you find that you're compromising your values to be with someone, this is a bad thing.

Does your new partner make you spend too much money? Or rush you into sex too fast, before you're really comfortable with it? Are you partying so hard every night it's hard to get to work in the morning? Are you associating with people you wouldn't otherwise, due to their bad characters and/or habits? If so, being single is better than what you're doing.

You stay too long

Has the relationship become obviously dysfunctional? When all you do is argue or clash (or worse) with your partner, there's no reason to stay. Some people do, out of fear of being single. But is it really worse than staying with someone who damages your self-esteem and who doesn't support you in any way?

Here again, being single is actually better. Don't let your desire for love and affection blind you to your own reality.

Signs of seduction

You may or may not have recognized yourself in the list above. But even if you're not easily seduced, you might still fall under someone's spell. Here are some signals to watch out for:

To begin with, you consent to the seduction. (Otherwise, if there's no consent, its rape.) We're not victim-blaming here. The key to seducing another is that the pursuer uses deceit and manipulation to obtain that consent. You didn't freely give it because your seducer was hiding their intentions from you. Moreover, you likely would not have consented if your pursuer hadn't lied or deceived you.

For example, you might not consent to sex unless you believed that the other person was in love with you, or at least willing to explore being in a long-term relationship with you. Knowing this, and also knowing that they had no desire for anything other than sex, your seducer may have led you to believe that they wanted a relationship with you. Had you known all they wanted was sex, you wouldn't have agreed to go to bed with them in the first place.

The seducer doesn't really care about their target and all they want is a boost to their ego or some personal pleasure out of the chase. While they may appear interested in order to further their pursuit, they're not particularly interested in anyone but themselves. This one might be a little harder to suss out because most seducers are skilled at pretending interest! Or, they may genuinely be interested so they can figure out which of your buttons are best to push.

Look at their actions. Do they remember the little, unimportant details that make you who you are and aren't about sex? Or is their interest geared mainly toward finding out what charms and entices you? When they talk about other people, is it in the service of themselves or do they seem curious about others? Are there other narcissistic tendencies that you spot? It's unethical to deceive someone into getting what you want, but many seducers use this ploy, especially in the romantic arena, where it's commonly believed that men want one thing and women another! This is not necessarily true. In a perfectly ethical world, both sides have the same information and consent is mutual. This is not the world we're living in, however.

Three-step model: attraction, comfort, and seduction

The first thing the seducer needs to do is to attract their target. Because they tend to be magnetic and charismatic, this is usually not the hard part for them! They know how to stand out in a crowd and draw attention to themselves. This is where the seduction begins, before they even approach the person they're interested in. All eyes are on them, which also makes them look popular and confident. Once they make direct contact, they'll make their target feel empowered and interesting. Being direct in their approach makes them look courageous. People like risk-takers, as they're a novelty.

Or they might try the indirect approach, which consists of asking an (apparently) random question. This maneuver is designed to smoothly engage in conversation. Whether the indirect or direct opener is used, the seducer normally pivots to wordplay, charm, and humor - all of which are known to attract others. Sometimes seducers, especially men, will open up a conversation with a woman they're not interested in. Once a man is seen talking to a woman, especially an attractive one, other women may be interested in him, as well. Interestingly, other species are known to perform this "mate choice copying",[13] in which females of the species copy other females in choosing a specific male for mating. But the seducer can't give too much away, upfront. No one wants the prize handed over to them on a silver platter. Once the target is hooked, they'll start withdrawing. This is confusing and intriguing, which keeps their target's attention. The relationship continues over time, as normally seduction doesn't occur all in one go. In order to keep the interest levels high, the seducer has to sustain some emotional tension - keeping their audience off-balance and wanting more.

Next is the building of the relationship. Comfort and trust with the pursuer have to be established before the target can be enticed into the seduction. Increased eye contact makes the pursued feel that the seducer is interested in them. The pursuer may also lean toward their target, decreasing the personal space between them. In addition to using wit, the seducer also uses the power of touch - not in a sexual way, at least at first. But humans respond with trust even with a brief touch of a hand. It promotes bonding between the two. The brain releases neurochemicals when the body is touched, including oxytocin, which is the bonding chemical.

---

[13] https://journals.sagepub.com/doi/full/10.1177/147470491201000511

Physical affection and rapport-building continues up to and during the seduction itself, to maintain the levels of trust necessary for the target to agree to have sex. The decision has to be made emotionally, not logically. The seducer will use words and body language for emotional appeal and emotional rapport. This is not trust built on similar experiences or values, but on a similar drive, both have (or the pursuer appears to have) to be in a physical and romantic relationship.

Chapter Summary

- Seducers have qualities that make them stand out from the ordinary, even if their charm and charisma are superficial.
- Some people are easily seduced because they're dissatisfied with their lives or have other unfulfilled needs that a seducer can exploit.
- Signs of seduction involve consent that appears mutual, but isn't, due to deceit on the part of the pursuer.
- The model of seduction encompasses three main stages: attraction, comfort and trust-building, and the seduction itself.

In the next chapter, you will learn the rules of the game of seduction.

CHAPTER FOUR:

The Rules of the Game

The art (and science) of seduction is really a game with two principal players. Others may be involved around the edges. When a man initiates a conversation with a woman he's not trying to entice, in order to attract another one that he does intend to seduce, minor players are involved. Typically, in a romantic seduction, it's played with two people.

Game types

There are three main types of game that can be played, at least when it comes to sexual seduction.

1. Direct

The direct conversation opener I talked about in the last chapter is most often used for this type of game. Here, the pursuer is up-front in their approach to the target. They're not using other women to draw their target in, but are coming to her directly and expressing their attraction. It doesn't mean being crude, necessarily, just expressing interest. For those who fear rejection, this might seem like a terrifying task! But, because it makes you look like a brave risk-taker, your target will probably find your confidence attractive.

This technique also means less manipulation and less knowledge about human nature because you're not trying to be sly about it or use some human characteristic to your advantage. At some point, you'll likely need to be direct in your approach anyway. Especially when you're "closing the deal" to have sex.

2. Indirect

By contrast, when you're playing an indirect game, you don't let your target know you're attracted until after they've already displayed some attraction to you. This skips over the potential of rejection that's always a possibility of the direct game. It's a strategy game in which you draw out your target to discover things about them and have them qualify themselves for sex with you. Once you've displayed a bit about yourself, to attract them, they then reveal more about themselves. You can test to see if they're actually interested in you before you let them know that you are sexually interested in them.

The problem with this type of game is that there's usually a sexual tension between the two sexes anyway. If you're going for the indirect technique, you have to maneuver yourself so they're not aware upfront of your sexual interest in them, yet keep the tension strong enough that you can attract them and then build the comfort level.

3. Social

When using the social game, you need to know about some human quirks in order to use them as leverage against your target. Here's where the "mate choice copy" technique might come in. Ideally, you want to enter the venue with a crowd of people and have your target wondering who you are. You don't have to be high-status to attract the one you want to seduce, but you do need to be confident and socialize.

Who are the players of the game?

In chapter two, I discussed the different types of seducers. There are various types of victims, as well. In general, they lack something that their seducer is able to exploit or use for leverage. The pursuer must be careful that they're reading their targets correctly, though. Most of us hide or at least try to hide our weaknesses and vulnerabilities. Someone who comes across as tough and strong might, in fact, be protecting a heart soft as a marshmallow!

Some victims are actually former seducers, who had to stop due to family or other pressures. They may be resentful or bitter about this change because they miss being able to seduce people. When you're pursuing them, though, remember that they need to think they're the ones seducing you, not the other way around. Other seducers have lived their life of pleasure and are feeling jaded. They can often be easily seduced by someone who appears young and innocent because it brings back memories of their own youth.

A target who fetishizes the exotic leads an empty inner life and wants to fill it up with exotic treats. An exotic pursuer fits the bill, especially if you exaggerate a bit. Those who are bored with their lives will fill it with drama, so don't chase a drama queen with the promise of safety and security. Other victims may be highly imaginative people who find that reality just doesn't match up to their fantasies. Spoiled children need novelty and the firm hand their parents never gave them. A target who doesn't want to grow up and take responsibility is also searching for a parent.

Someone who was once a star (athlete, student, actor, whatever), who now leads a drab existence, will absolutely perk up once someone lavishes some attention on them. Likewise, someone who's beautiful or especially handsome is always worried they're losing their looks. Seduce them by paying homage to their looks, but also to another characteristic (like brains, wit, or personality) that no one else has paid much attention to. You might find a target who acts like they're whiter than snow, but deep down, they're both terrified of and titillated by the thought of forbidden pleasures in the bedroom. Others are under no illusion about their actual purity, but they also want to taste these as-yet-untasted fruits.

People who are power-hungry need to release some energy, so being a tease works very well for them. Some leaders are genuinely powerful, but because they are leaders, they need someone to break down their walls for them and end their isolation. Others hide their need for power under the guise of being a rescuer. Other targets may have spent so much time in their heads and working on their (perceived) mental superiority that a physical pursuer comes as something of a relief to them. They also tend to be insecure underneath, so you can play on that, too. Some victim's inner voids are so huge that they try to fill it with worship: a cause, a religion, or an idol. Their minds are overactive and they're also physically understimulated. For someone whose senses are overstimulated, they actually need more sensual pleasures, as they tend to be shy.

If someone's gender is fluid or ambiguous, they're most likely looking for another gender fluid person to stir up some of their repressed desires.

Is seduction ethically responsible?

Some states in the US, at least at one time, made certain types of (sexual) seduction illegal.[14] If a man tricked a woman by promising marriage or used other trickery, and if the woman was under 25 or previously a virgin or the man was over a specific age, the seduction could be rendered a crime. In the modern world, however, women have more agency and so seduction isn't a crime. Although many people still view it as immoral, there's definitely a case to be made for ethical seduction!

Avoiding total lies and false impressions is important. If you have no intention of marrying your conquest, don't promise a wedding. And don't give off the impression that you're willing to consider a wedding, either. If you're trying to charm someone into having sex with you, make it clear that your end result is sex, not a trip down the aisle or a long-term relationship. Not only is this the ethical way to do it, it also shortens the

---

[14] https://www.britannica.com/topic/seduction

process of getting into bed. In popular culture, the woman who is marriage material doesn't have sex until much later in the relationship. When she knows that marriage isn't in the cards, she doesn't need to act like marriage material and she doesn't need to keep putting up obstacles between you and sex. And if you don't know her very well, how would you know if she was someone you wanted to marry in the first place? Acting like she's marriage material right away is dishonest because you'd need to get to know her better in the first place.

An obviously immoral way to seduce someone is to use your power or status. The "casting couch" in Hollywood, though it's been used a lot, is unethical. If you're someone's boss and you require them to go to bed with you to keep their job, this is not seduction at all. It's a pure power play and there's nothing alluring or enticing about it.

However, what if you were to do things right? Treat your partner as a whole person that you're attracted to? Everyone finds that approach charming! Knowing what your target responds to isn't manipulative because everyone does it. The power relationship is equal - most people figure out this aspect of human nature pretty quickly if they don't already know it when they begin dating. With an ethical seduction, there's still plenty of flirting, teasing, and wordplay involved, if both partners enjoy it. But, the pursuer makes clear what they're after and the target picks up on these signals and responds in kind. When the response is positive, the seducer can then start making the moves to close the deal and end the journey with sex. If the response is negative, the pursuer may change targets and begin again.

Everyone involved in this type of seduction has realistic expectations about what is happening. No one gets hurt because they don't have false hopes that end up clashing with reality. Both parties are attracted to each other. There's no reason to ramp up one's attractiveness with artifice or game-playing. Consent is mutually given because both parties are clear about what's expected.

Drawing the line

In the online seduction community, some men have no desire to be "pick-up artists" who have sex with women and then discard them because they can. These men are just looking for dating advice, so they can have better dates and more sex. There's nothing necessarily immoral or unethical about this. But where should the line be drawn? Some of the seduction techniques come from NLP (neuro-linguistic programming), which is thought to enhance communication techniques. It's also often considered to be deceitful and manipulative because the people using it aren't open about it. Is it abuse if you have a lot of seductive power and you use it to your advantage? As noted above, seduction can be manipulative and have destructive consequences.

Sexual harassment happens with both male and female supervisors. If the employer is using their hiring and firing power to force an employee into sex, that's coercive and not seductive.

Chapter Summary

- There are three types of seductive games people play: direct, indirect, and social - each of which has its advantages, disadvantages, and techniques.
- There are many different types of targets that seducers will find easy to pursue, especially if they understand human nature and the various ways in which people experience a lack of something in their lives.
- Seduction doesn't have to be manipulative and deceitful, as long as the seducer makes their intentions clear.
- Using one's power and status to coerce someone else into having sex is a clear line between seduction and lack of consent.

In the next chapter, you will learn about the art of seduction.

CHAPTER FIVE:

The Art of Seduction

Anyone who takes the time to learn this art can be a master (or mistress) of the seduction game. It combines a knowledge of human nature with historical experience obtained over centuries. You'll need to know the type of seducer that you most resemble and uncover the strategies that will work for you and your specific type. If you resonated with any of the victim types discussed in chapter three, stay away from them as your targets!

An introduction to the techniques of seduction

People like mystery and uncertainty. It keeps them drawn in, wanting to find out what happens next. If you've chosen your target correctly, they'll be doing their best to uncover your mystery and take you for themselves. Competition is also seductive. Develop the charisma that leaves your targets wanting more. You'll need to appear confident because that's another characteristic that hooks people easily. Hook them, but don't let them get too close to you. Distance gives you the mythic aura you want to cultivate.

Be the hero or heroine of a great drama, but remember, as with all heroes, you can't get too close to the common people. Stay up on that pedestal as long as you can. Act as if your power is innate and a gift of creation. Hard work and discipline is a boner-killer when it comes to seduction. Don't let on that you've been practicing and studying. Whatever type of seducer you are, you want it to appear effortless. After all, anybody can put in hard work to achieve a goal, but a successful seducer is not just anyone! They're a rare being with a huge presence that others are attracted to, but can't necessarily get close to, at least not until the seducer lets their target in. There eventually should be a touch of vulnerability - just a touch - being needy turns most people right off. This allows the pursued to feel special because they're the ones allowed to touch the hem of the seducer's garment.

The keys to seduction lie in your ability to show charisma, even if you don't necessarily think of yourself as naturally charismatic. You must be confident and act like you have a plan. Be mysterious enough that you intrigue others. Pull them in, then push them back. Make your target work for the opportunity to be seduced by you because people don't trust gifts given too freely.

Phases of seduction and their techniques

We've discussed the overall journey of seduction: attraction, comfort and rapport-building, and the actual seduction. Let's go into the seduction phases in more detail and discuss the strategies that go along with each.

Cut the target out of the pack and incite desire and attraction

You'll need to select your target carefully to make sure they fit in with your type and that you can address the void they have within themselves. Ignore the ones who aren't attracted to you or who you can't appeal to because they're just a waste of your time. Show that you're the seducer by being choosy. There may be a number of people who seem open to your charms, but you don't need to take the first one on offer. This would be a move based on insecurity, not confidence, so it will eventually backfire. You might choose someone who seems shy because they often respond well to being approached and would like to be drawn out. Your target shouldn't seem to be too busy. Too much work on your part and they won't have the time to spend with you that you need to be successful in your seduction.

Once you've selected a good target who's ready for you, start making conversation. Get to know a little about them so you can use that information for later, especially little tidbits about their youth or childhood, or something about what makes them tick. Once they're comfortable talking to you, you can make an unusual or surprising suggestion - something they find intriguing. You don't want to pay them too much attention, at first. Remember how attractive distance is. Once you've made the approach and intrigued them, you want them to come to you. They want to feel like the seducer, not the seduced. Backing off also lets them use their imaginations a little bit. That's more alluring than spelling everything out for them. Send mixed or ambiguous signals. Most people are so obvious that you'll come across as more interesting. You must also let them know you have complexity that can't be addressed in one initial meeting. They'll need to get to know you better to uncover this intriguing and mysterious quality. If you present as innocent and cherubic, you'll need to let out a hint of cruelty or danger to keep them interested.

Playing on vanity can provide great rewards! If you're interested in a specific person, flirt with their friend. This is one way to create a "triangle of desire", which is an excellent way to lure in your target. Women especially are attracted to men with a "rakish reputation", so use that to your advantage. While you're in the first phase of seduction, you'll be planting seeds for later. One seed is to make them worried about the future. Bring up in them the doubts and securities you learned in your conversation. This prepares the ground for your second seed of insinuation, which is that you'll be able to address this void in their life. This is a good time to play along with them. What a coincidence that you enjoy what they enjoy! You adapt to their mood, which plays to their ego.

Unsettle them with confusion and pleasure

Creating suspense is key! Do things they don't expect from you, which keeps them coming back for more. They want to know what happens next and you don't want to make that too obvious. People love novelty, so attract them with it, but also use it to keep them off-balance.

Remember to add in that little touch of vulnerability from time to time and strategically show a little weakness or vulnerability. Avoid doing it accidentally because you'll come off as insecure or confident. Decide what weakness you'll let them taste and when. Make it enough to make them feel superior or strong, at least for a brief time. It should be natural to your character, so even though you're using it in a calculated way, it won't appear calculating.

Don't be reliable. If you choose, for example, to send them a letter or flowers, don't do that on a regular basis. You want them panting after you, not the other way around. Use your words! Seduction is about emotional appeal. Flatter, use heavily loaded language, appeal to their vanity, ego, and self-esteem. Wrap them in fantasies and rich, imaginary worlds. They won't have the will to resist when you're using language as leverage. You'll need to pay attention to detail, so you know which buttons to push. Be poetic, be vulgar (if your target is OK with it), naughty, or sensuous, but don't be ordinary. Embody their fantasies. In your conversations, hopefully, you discovered what it is they're looking for. Now, you want to blur the lines between fantasy and reality by being that fantasy figure they've been dreaming of for so long. All this will help you isolate them from their natural environment: physical, mental, emotional, encouraging them to depend more on you than they have yet.

Deepen the effect and push them onto the ledge

Show your target that you are the embodiment of their dreams, according to the seed you planted. If you're playing the white knight, now is the time to manufacture a drama or crisis (if there isn't one already), so you can swoop in and fulfill their fantasies of being rescued, for example. Whatever type of seducer you are, don't worry about looking silly or making a mistake. Anything that looks like a sacrifice is going to impress your target and reinforce the idea that you're their dream lover in the flesh.

People love to feel like they're exploring their dark side. You might help them push past self-imposed limits, or maybe limits put in place by society. Either way, let them feel like you're leading them to transgress and explore something they have always wanted but never dared. Normally, this will be sexual in nature! You can engage in behavior that's forbidden to most, which makes you dangerously enticing. Allow your target to enjoy the lure of the forbidden.

Make sure, whether you're seducing someone who's vain about their appearance or not, that you express attraction beyond the physical. Many people have insecurities and worries about their bodies and you don't want those anxieties to scare them off. Make them so aware of their weakness that they can't concentrate on you. Express your appreciation for something that's not physical. Appeal to something sublime to redirect them, like religion or the occult, or even an amazing work of art. The key to this phase is not to focus exclusively on pleasure. You lure them in with your promise of being the hero, or heroine. Once you've paid attention to them, you want to back off abruptly. Interested, interested, interested...now bring the pain. Suddenly, you're no longer attracted to them. You can even drive yourselves into a breakup, so they feel the emptiness in their lives without you. Then you can bring back the pleasure, until you need to ratchet up some more tension and back off once more.

Don't avoid conflict. You'll need to maintain the sexual tension and that's not possible without some conflict. Pull them in and push them away and repeat. Vary the times you spend in pleasure and in pain, so it's not boring or predictable. Maybe this breakup is for real! You don't want them to figure out a pattern.

Push them off and move in

Introduce some jealousy into the equation. As usual, nothing too obvious. Drop some hints about your possible interest in another person, then let your target's imagination run wild. Willpower is linked to sexual libido in a way that you can easily exploit. If they're waiting for you to come to them - if they believe they're being pursued - the sexual temperature is low. Raise it up by inciting some new emotions, tension, and jealousy. Get them involved in the pursuit, instead of relaxing and waiting for you. While they're getting hotter and hotter, you're totally nonchalant. After all, everyone expects the hero or heroine to be cool, calm, and collected. Meanwhile, you're watching for signs of their libido warming up. They might start blushing, even crying. Keep an eye out for revealing slips of the tongue, too. These are all signs that they're ready for you to close the deal.

You are the pursuer, even if they mistakenly think that they're chasing you. This also means you're the one who has to make the bold move. It's up to you, but you still must maintain your aura of cool and mystery. You're making the move, but you can't be desperate for their response. Afterward, you might still need to stir the pot to maintain your elusiveness. But when you are done or disenchanted, make sure you end it. Don't continue out of pity or because you don't have anyone else. Make a clean break if you can. If you can't, get them to break up with you by deliberately using some anti-seductive behavior.

Seduction notes for beginners

There are a few things you need to know to get you up to speed. They'll also help you master the art of seduction.

Turn off your phone

In order to maintain your focus on learning and seduction, you need to avoid distractions. Being too immersed in your phone means that you will be too easily turned away from your goals by an ill-timed notification or text message. Plus, your potential targets will be insulted, not attracted, when you start looking at your phone as you're speaking to them. Staying away from your phone helps you get into a flow state, in which you're focused on what you're doing. Flow states are key for creativity, too.

Study

Watch what successful seducers are doing. Watch how they play the game. Reading about them in this book gives you a good background, but you'll help your game leap forward by watching what works out in the world and copying it. Find a mentor if you can. They also can help you make the most of your seducer personality and give you some tips and tricks on how they do what they do. You can also YouTube or search well-known charmers and watch them online.

Visualize

You can do this "in the field", as well as at other times. Visualization is a mindset trick that successful athletes and business people all use. What does a successful night in the field look like? Why are you trying to improve your seduction game and what is your goal? Whatever it is, play it as it lays. When you're about to set out for the night, imagine in your mind how you want the night to go. Picture how you will find an appropriate target and how you'll slide into conversation with them.

Consistent practice

Like so many other journeys in life, seduction and improving your game are endurance contests. They are marathons, not sprints. So don't wear yourself out practicing too much in a short period of time and then needing too much time to recover. Instead, practice a bit each day. Some days you might only take 10 minutes, other times you might be able to work on it for an hour. Don't overwhelm yourself with too much too soon. Take it easy enough that you actually have time to improve, as well as time to reflect and learn from each practice session.

System of learning from your practice

For most people, this practice will be in the form of "field notes". Once you return home from a practice session, relive the night. Write it down because leaving it in your head means you won't get the full power of reflection. When you're writing, take special note of what went well.

Did you say something that piqued your target's interest, or did you try a casual touch to increase bonding? Also, take note of what didn't go well. Maybe your indirect game was a little too indirect and didn't let the target understand your attraction.

What was going on in the outside world where you practiced? What was going on internally? Did anything trigger your insecurities and were you able to handle them or do you need a game plan in case it happens again? What do you want to try again? Is there something new you might want to test out? Or something that in your opinion failed so badly you never want to use it again? Most mentors will want to hear your notes.

Balance between too easy and too hard

If you're only practicing the easy stuff, like approaching targets who appear desperate for some interaction, you won't improve. You'll stay mediocre and won't be able to master your game. On the other hand, if you're constantly aiming too high beyond your current abilities, you won't really know what went well and what didn't. You just don't know enough to make that determination and you won't be able to improve by constantly going too hard, either. Plus, it's very easy to get discouraged when you're aiming at the impossible because you'll be failing.

Limit what you want to focus on in each session and that way you'll be able to learn more quickly.

Sleep

Brains need rest! Cell repair and other processes can only take place when you're asleep, so you need to make sure you're taking time for sleep. Learning happens during sleep too, as memories and experiences get encoded. Nap if you need to, so you can stay up late and practice your game later at night.

Chapter Summary

- Seduction involves art and techniques that have been acquired over centuries.
- Each phase of the seduction contains techniques applicable to that phase, no matter what type of seducer you are.
- You can improve your game faster with a few hacks, including consistent practice and taking notes on your practice sessions.

In the next chapter, you will learn seduction techniques in more detail.

CHAPTER SIX:

Seduction Techniques 101

Here, I'll discuss the techniques that men use to sexually seduce women. Just a reminder that these are based on centuries of knowledge and experience, including what men have discovered about how women work and how to leverage that information into seduction.

Introduction to the best techniques men use to seduce women

There are a couple of common maneuvers that men have used successfully to entice women into bed. One is acting like a Player or Casanova, meaning that you're known for your amorous pursuits and you're very smooth and debonair about it. You ardently love 'em, and then you leave 'em. If you're a Player, you know you have skills that other men don't have. Generally, you have your pick of the women you want because you use these smooth maneuvers and strategies. The media makes the single life, at least for men, fun and glamorous. Settling down is perceived to be boring and sometimes even the death of sex. Who wouldn't want to be out there flirting with a different woman every night?

Players usually don't bring their women into their lives. They have so many they don't want to keep introducing new people to their friends and family. They're confident and allow the ball to fall into their target's court, so the target can pursue them instead. Their ultimate goal is sex, as quickly as possible.

There are several different types of Players. They might be the only decent-looking and/or single guy in their office or town, so women flock to them! Others are known for how much attention they pay to the opposite sex, plying them with drinks, compliments, and teddy bears. Or a man might play the mystery card, where he lets drop little hints about his life and the complexities of being him…but no one gets all the information, even though all the women are trying to find out! And, of course, there's the bad boy who's hard to predict and never dull. When people talk about him being the bad boy, women line up at the door to try to prove them wrong. They won't. He really won't find a long-term relationship that he wants to be in.

No matter what kind of Player appeals to you, it means being super cool and playing by your own rules. You can't be like all the other guys, or else you'll blend into the crowd. Women want someone who dares to be different. Show them that you're different. In being cool, you do need to be above it all. No one responds well to desperation, so get them curious about you. Intrigue them, but don't give them what they want right away. Keep them hooked. Playing hard to get works for you in this situation. People always want what they can't have, so let your target know they can't have you and watch them try!

Women like a man who's witty. If a man speaks quickly enough and in monotone, he can induce a near-trance in his target. This is one of the advantages of neuro-linguistic programming or NLP. A Player works with all their senses, not just words, but scent, sight, and touch. He'll appeal to her brains, too, and ask her what she thinks. He can be playful and definitely unpredictable. He might surprise her with gifts or take her somewhere spontaneously. A good seducer has several language tricks up his sleeve, in addition to being smart and charming. He can act like the hero that will wipe her tears away. If the woman is having problems in her current relationship, the seducer can talk about how sad she looks and seems.

The converse of this is acting like you need her protection, her shoulder to cry on. You're having problems in a current relationship, which may or may not be a romantic one. But it could be a problem at work or with friends, too. You're showing some vulnerability and making her feel like the strong one. Acting like a romantic man is also a great way to lure in the target. Citing classical quotes or reading her poetry is a trick most women fall for. Paying attention to what the target wants will help you determine whether she's a "bad girl" or a good one. But, whichever one she is...play to the opposite. If she's a good girl, she wants to be bad, or at least taste some forbidden fruit. If she's a bad girl, she wants romance. When you're attuned to the details, you'll be able to do something special for her that she appreciates and she'll begin letting down her guard.

You might even try starting a rumor about yourself! Something calculated to appeal, or something that a woman will be inclined to defend you on. As with all seduction techniques, be deliberate about it. Don't accidentally let go of some information about yourself, or allow someone else to start rumors. Calculate your approach and your maneuvers.

You can be an asshole and seduce plenty of women, but you have to be genuine about it - uncaring. You're an asshole because you don't care about the results, or about society or rules. But if you're spiteful because you're reacting to something you care about, you won't be able to attract women. Aloofness works well, especially with women.

Right now you might be wondering why being a Player and an indifferent asshole works so well when luring women to your bed. It's called the "sexy sons" hypothesis.[15] Women want to have sons who will be attractive to the opposite sex, so they will have sex with men who are attractive to other women. It's thought that female orgasm is a way to make fertilizing the egg more likely. Evolution directs orgasm to occur with more desirable mates. In this context, "desirable" means possessing the genes that women want to pass on to their potential sons in order for them to attract desirable women. Research has found that women have more orgasms with men who other women also find attractive, which helps validate the sexy sons' hypothesis.

---

[15] https://www.psychologytoday.com/intl/blog/slightly-blighty/201508/the-sexy-sons-theory-what-women-are-attracted-in-men

Mind games and covert seduction

The previous suggestions were a little obvious, but now we're going to delve into more of the activities that may not be as clear to both participants of the game. These types of games use the target's mind against her a bit more than the others you've read about so far.

Cold reading

One way to start messing with a woman's mind is to try "cold reading", which is the same tactic that many so-called mediums and mind readers use. You'll need to be able to read female body language pretty well to make this tactic work. In it, you make suggestions that apply to many women and let her mind and imagination do the rest. It's especially effective if you read her palm because you then get to let the sense of touch work its magic, too. Whether or not you're doing the cold reading, make sure you stay playful and interesting.

What are the basics of a cold read? Whether you're playing the seduction game or setting yourself out as a medium or tarot card reader, you're operating on the same basic set of assumptions - that people are more alike than they are different and major life events are the same for all: birth, puberty, work, marriage, having a child, aging, and dying. People don't visit cold readers because they're happy, but because they're trying to solve a problem. Most of the time, these problems are due to love, money, health, or the lack thereof. A good cold reader, one that can make a living at it, has a keen eye for detail. They notice jewelry, skin, clothing, and other accessories that tell them what the problem is likely to be. You may not have this eye for detail or even care very much about it. But most people, even if we have different goals and aspirations, share the same outlook on life. A lot of beliefs are driven by culture, so if you know the woman's culture, you probably already know a lot about her beliefs and outlook.

As it turns out, you can do pretty well even with a "stock spiel", as long as it's vague enough that it covers a large number of women. The best ones are about three-quarters positive, with about a quarter of the reading negative.[16] As long as you're confident and act like you know what you're doing, your target will probably be convinced that you have accurately read her and she'll be amazed at what you know. This works because when someone hears potentially contradictory statements, their brains immediately start trying to make sense of things. Put them together in some sort of coherent fashion. Good vague tactics to use include talking about different parts of her. You can contrast two parts: "Your smile is so innocent, but I can see something darker in your eyes." Or sometimes they're one way - say, adventurous and bold - and other times they're timid and don't want to take risks. Since this applies to most people, it's pretty safe to say! If you know some basic body language tidbits, you can use those, too. "I know you're emotionally closed off because you're standing there with your arms crossed over your chest."

Start your cold reading playfully. You might even tell her you're psychic, to get her intrigued. Or, you can start with a general statement that's probably true and go from there. You want to bring in her emotions, so you might start with a "negative" emotion, like anxiety, and then tell her something positive about it. Once you've done some generic cold reads, use a touchier one, like the "closed-off" example above. The women you cold-read will be surprised by how much you know, which lets their defenses down, so you can learn quite a bit about them at a deeper level than with some other techniques. Since you already know so much about them, it's not a big deal for them to confess deeper vulnerabilities. This allows you to connect with your target, especially if she's conventionally attractive and only used to men commenting on her looks. You can add in some statements about sex or repression to get her thinking about your ultimate goal, even if unconsciously.

The more cold reading you do, the easier it will become. With a glance, you'll be able to read your targets and show them your amazing power. It's a great way to build rapport while you're making her feel comfortable with you because you'll "discover" things that the two of

---

[16] https://heartiste.net/cold-reading-is-a-potent-seduction-tactic/

you have in common. Cold reading is probably not going to get a woman to go all the way to bed with you, so you'll need to use some other methods, too. But it's a quick way to get a woman's attention and show her some unusual powers, unless she identifies as a skeptic, in which case she'll mess with you as you attempt your reading! You may also find as you discover more about her that you don't really want to spend more time with her and can gracefully make an exit!

Hover and disqualify

Another tactic is known as "hover and disqualify". You can probably guess what it means! The benefit is that it can work no matter your level of game, or what type of seducer personality is closest to yours.

First, you get near your target physically, so she has to see you. Best not to do this in a creepy way, but find a (plausible) reason to be in her vicinity. If she's standing at the bar, you have the built-in excuse of buying a drink. If she's standing off somewhere else, you might pull out your phone and pretend to check it. Don't get so lost in your notifications that you forget why you picked that particular spot! Don't face her, but it's best to be in a position so that you can see what she's doing, in case you see a good time to approach. This is the "hover" part.

Next, you want to appear to disqualify her as a potential partner by overtly checking out another woman while you're standing near your target. This will incite some jealousy and heat her up a bit. You'll need to ensure that she sees you checking out the other women, so you may need to be more overt instead of subtle here. If another woman has a terrific butt, make an obvious show of checking out that butt.

The "hover and disqualify" technique does a few things for you. First, because you're not looking directly at your target, you don't seem to be too interested in her, or too needy. Standing near her but looking at other women sends mixed signals. People find these signals confusing and enticing, so the more you send the better! Jealousy is a sexy emotion and your target may see your attention to another woman as a challenge to her. Women love challenges! Once you've executed the technique, you can approach your intended target. You can do it right away, if the opportunity presents itself, and you can do it smoothly. Otherwise, you may have to walk away for a short period and then return.

There are a few things to be careful of with this technique, or it might not work. Don't look at the "disqualifier" for too long, or you'll seem creepy. Notice her, check out an obviously attractive feature, but then look away after you're sure your target has noticed. It's also possible that your target will be so self-conscious that she doesn't rise to the occasion: she allows herself to be DQ'd without putting up a fight or resistance against it. You can try showing her a bit more attention if this happens, but you may just need to move on.

Negging

The technique you've most likely heard of in relation to being a pick-up artist is "negging". You aim a mild insult (too mild to cause much offense) at a woman, which is surprising because men don't typically do that to women they want to have sex with! The element of surprise is a novelty that the human brain craves. Women, particularly very attractive ones, aren't used to anything but praise. You'll stand out in a crowd using this tactic. Negging expresses a mild disinterest in the woman, which again is unusual and attention-getting. It puts you in control of the situation. Now she's trying to earn your approval, as the result of the back-handed compliment you gave her, rather than the other way around. Even if you don't consider yourself a pick-up artist, you might use negging to spice up your interactions a little bit.

Negging should be used carefully. It's intended for women who are physically very attractive because, for them, a backhanded compliment is unusual. For women who are not conventionally attractive, it may not be so much of a novelty. When done in a matter-of-fact way, it doesn't work very well because women find it so creepy. It's best used after a little flirtation and back-and-forth with the woman and said in a flirty or playful tone, as well.

Social proof

The tactic of social proof is also a good one to use, no matter how much you've practiced seduction. It's based on the assumption most people make that if many people are making a certain choice, it has to be the correct option. For example, which restaurant do you go to? The one that has no customers, or the one that's bustling with diners? You go to the busy one because you assume there must be something wrong with the other one if no one's eating there.

This even works with things like choosing to go to college. If you live in a place where no one goes to college after they've finished high school, you probably won't go either. On the other hand, if everyone you know goes to college, you're likely to attend, as well. When are you going to buy an online course: when you see an ad that looks good and tells you how good the course is, or when your friends told you what a difference the course made in their lives? Naturally, you'll go with your friends' recommendations.

How does this work in the seduction scene? Social proof is when you're surrounded by other women or known to have had sex with other women. They want to be with you, so your target will recognize that she needs to choose you because you're the socially correct option.

There are three main ways that you can build social proof, relatively quickly. One is to be seen in the company of other women. This works best if your crowd is attractive, young women. It still works if you have a cool friend and you're hanging out with him and his squad. You'll get some spillover effect. You can also approach another woman or group of women and start talking to them in an animated way and, at some point, excuse yourself to have a conversation with your target. This is a little bit like disqualifying, but not quite the same.

The second way is to be a social butterfly and work the room. The more people you meet, the more people want to meet you. That's just how the social animal goes. When people want to talk to you, you'll come off as high-status. You must really be "somebody" if everyone wants to meet you! You'll be intriguing and women will want to get to know you. The downside to this type of social proof is that it's too easy to slide into entertainer mode and forget the reason you're here. Or you'll be on such a manic high energy that you won't be able to pull it back to be cool and indifferent when you need to approach a woman.

Keep moving in the crowd until you find a woman that you do want to get to know better. Don't get stuck talking to someone who isn't interesting (male or female) for too long. But, once you do find that intriguing woman, you need to have the wherewithal to stop your flitting around and work on her.

Finally, find a place where you're known. If you don't have one already, you can find one for yourself. You'll want a bar or nightclub where you can get to know the staff and regulars. It should also be a place where there's plenty of turnover, meaning new women appear consistently. You don't want to pick a place where you'll only be seeing the same faces every time you go because your game will wear very thin, very quickly. It should also be a place where women are looking to meet new partners, not a coffee shop or tearoom where they go to hang out with friends. They should be coming to this place with the idea that they'll find a man to have some sexual or romantic time with. The venue ideally has little nooks or tables where you can bring a woman to get away from the high energy and focus on your seduction. Best of all is a place that has different floors and distinct spaces, so you can change venues without leaving.

To build up your cred once you've found such a place, go to it consistently. Just as with your practice sessions, you don't have to spend a long time while you're here, but you need to make regular appearances. To get to know the staff, it's best to get here a little early or at off times, so they're not too busy to spend some time with you. Get comfortable with it and explore all it has to offer. You want to know where you can take a woman for some seductive one-on-one time. Study it, so you know when the women typically arrive and can be there for the newbies.

Kino-escalation

Ever heard of kino-escalation? It relies on the erotic power of touch to help you connect with the woman you want to have sex with. Recall that touch helps release the bonding neurotransmitter oxytocin. Touching a woman says a lot about you, all of which is good. It shows that you're confident and not worried about whether you'll scare her off. It demonstrates that you're a physical type of guy. Women find confident men who aren't afraid to use touch very sexy. Just as with your speech, you need to touch a woman with self-assurance and make it deliberate. Otherwise, you'll seem unsure, which is a definite turnoff.

When you start off at night, you'll often need to lean in close and touch, in order for her to be able to hear what you're saying. But, if you're starting with touch during the day, you can't whisper in her ear when you first meet, it's too creepy. Adjust accordingly.

It's much harder to seduce a woman when you don't use kino-escalation. Touch is very powerful! If she gives you positive signals, you can keep going. These are demonstrated by her leaning into you and maybe even reciprocating the touch. If she's neutral, she won't move or touch you back. If the response is negative, she'll pull away from you. If you receive a neutral or negative signal, it doesn't necessarily mean that you should give up. She's not comfortable with you right now, so back off and give it some time before you try again. If she sends you a signal that you went too far, you can calmly and deliberately back off. Don't yank your hand back like you touched something hot because that also reads as not being confident. Even with touch, you shouldn't be consistent or predictable. If she's demonstrating that she likes a certain way you're touching her, stop for a bit. You'll begin again later.

When you're touching, don't be ham-handed about it. Light touches are the way to go - her arm briefly when you want to make a point, your knee against hers when you're crowded together. Don't leave your hand on her like a dead weight. You can break into the kino by touching her on the shoulder as a sign of approval. It's not sexual, but it is touch, and it leads the way for more to follow. When you lead her from one place to another, hold her hand. Recall earlier that a good place for you to be known is one that has separate spaces. It's a great idea to move her from one venue to another and you can hold her hand while you do it.

Once you've started more of a conversation, your touching can be a bit longer: hugging, stroking. Hold her by the waist, especially at a nightclub when you're struggling to talk over the music. The bonus to holding her waist is that you can gauge whether it's OK to go in for a kiss. Even a kiss is kino. Kiss the same way you're doing the rest of your touching: deliberately and with no hesitation. If she pulls back, let her go, and try again a bit later if she's signaling you to go for it.

Nightclubs are great for dancing. Many women love to dance and you can hold her hand as you lead her out to the floor. Dancing also allows you to be physically much closer to her and to touch her more intimately.

As long as it's okay at your venue, you can escalate to groping and making out eventually, as she becomes more comfortable with you. But if you can't close the deal, it's a bad idea. She'll cool off and recognize what you're trying to do, rather than staying caught up in the moment. If you can get her to the location, making out is an excellent way to escalate in terms of touch. You want her just dying to get into your pants, so turn her on with touch. Kiss her neck, play with her thighs, and use your fingers to great effect.

The key with kino is to escalate. Start small, with light brushes of her shoulder or arms. If you go too heavy too fast, you'll turn her off. Watch for her responses: if she wants you to back off, do it smoothly and deliberately. Give it a few moments before you go in again and you may want to start off with light touches (minor kino) first. Make sure she's comfortable with the light touches before you move to the medium (medium kino). And, again before you have sex (major kino). All phases must be respected or you'll be rejected for going too fast too soon.

Female psychology and the Shogun method: An overview

The next chapter delves more deeply into the Shogun method, but you should know that you can use female psychology to get her to be interested in you. It involves making her happy, but she also has to go through extremely negative experiences with you.

If you're a guy who doesn't mind sleeping around, you don't mind using mind control techniques, and you're OK with making a woman suffer a little bit in order for her to be yours, you should consider the Shogun method. It's a bit controversial and may be considered manipulative, but if that's OK with you, it could work. If you're either a psychopath who likes hurting women or your goal is to sleep with as many women as you possibly can until the day you die, you should move on to another technique.

Chapter Summary

- There are common tricks that work for men to seduce women, among them, being a Player or Casanova.
- More covert operations include mind games, like negging, cold reading, and "hover and disqualify".
- A more potent seduction technique is the Shogun method of making women suffer mentally in order to be yours.

In the next chapter, you will learn all about the Shogun method and other more devious seduction tactics.

CHAPTER SEVEN:

Devious Tactics of Seduction

So far, the techniques we've discussed have been a bit more innocuous. Yes, they're mind games, but the woman still has the choice of backing off or not being compliant. There are some more devious ways to seduce a woman, that involve more manipulation and deceit. In these techniques, consent isn't necessarily entirely mutual, because she may not be aware of what you're doing. But they will last longer and be more permanent, compared to some of the pick-up artist strategies that are designed for the short term.

Shogun method

When you use this tactic, you've crossed over the line and moved from seduction into enslavement. The trick here is to isolate the woman and separate her from her family and friends, so she ends up depending on you. (Remember you don't want to use this if all you really want to do is love 'em and leave 'em!)

There's a step-by-step roadmap that must be followed in order for the Shogun method to work, known as the IRAE roadmap. These letters stand for Intrigue, Rapport, Attract, and finally, Enslave. First, intrigue her and next, build rapport. Once you do this successfully, she'll then be attracted to you. Then, and only then can you mentally enslave her, which is a total emotional addiction to you, for life. If you try to do these steps out of order, it doesn't work. If you try to build rapport without intriguing her, you won't have a deep enough foundation with her. And there can't be a deep enough attraction without rapport-building and so on.

The PUA community puts the emphasis on men's inner game, but the Shogun method exploits weaknesses in women's psychology. Shogun sequences are designed to command her attention and lure her to make the choices you want her to make. This is all based on science - not movie-style mind control, but principles based on what we know about the brain, including NLP and applied psychology. Studies show that women can be polygamous and also hypergamous: they'll "mate-switch" if a better male than the one they currently have comes along. This is an opportunity for a willing Shogun practitioner, though also a risk.

This method can help men move out of the friend zone, recover after heartbreak and start over, and even bring back an ex they don't want to let go. Followers of the method say that you don't necessarily need to know a lot about women, as long as you take the steps as directed and have a basic understanding of the science, it will work.

Each of the stages in IRAE has its own sequences, or patterns, to help you draw the woman in:

During the Intrigue stage, you want her to be enticed by you. One sequence is to anchor the feelings she has for some object to you, as well. Identify her passion and have her transfer it to you. If she has a higher power or believes in such things, you can use it to create intrigue in her mind. Ask her about love and relationships. If she's a beautiful woman, let her know that you're interested in something more about her than just her looks.

Rapport-building is similar to techniques used in the pick-up artist scene. But you'll go a bit deeper than they do. You'll find her hidden weakness and show that you're the solution to her emptiness. All human beings have a need to belong to a group and so you'll create a shared group that consists only of the two of you.

Once you've built this deep rapport, it's time to move on to the Attraction stage. Building on your shared world, you'll show her how similar the two of you are. Invoke her dream guy, showing his similarities to you...and her current boyfriend's vast difference compared to the dream guy (if she currently has a BF that you need to be rid of). Then you'll show her that you're the perfect boyfriend.

The Enslavement stage has two phases. The first is where you isolate your target from her current environment, so she becomes dependent on you. Then, you use the Black Rose sequence, explained below, to erase her current identity and replace it with one that's subservient to you. This stage is not possible if you haven't gone through the previous three.

Implanted commands

As you're probably well aware, no one, including women, responds well to direct commands. But what if you planted a seed in the subconscious? This is the technique behind implanted commands. Instead of commanding her to do something directly, you camouflage it in such a way that she'll be charmed into it. You do have a direct command in your statement, which is what gets implanted, but you're not giving an actual order.

Here's an example: "I could tell you to commit to me, but someone like you needs to consider everything carefully before you make the right choice." "Commit to me" is the direct command, but that's not what she hears. And yet, that's what her subconscious absorbs.

Fractionation

Freud initially discovered this psychological tactic.[17] It uses hypnosis, persuasion, and psychology to uncover the secrets of a particular brain. It can be used during any of the IRAE stages. Typically in the seduction community, fractionation is a combination of hypnosis and the effective use of body language to make an emotional connection

---

[17] https://sibg.com/using-fractionation-in-seduction/

with the woman. You put her into a trance and remove her from it, repeatedly, leading to her emotional addiction to you.

If you're concerned about ethics, salespeople and Hollywood do this, too! They put you into the trance, snap you back into reality, and put you under again. In this technique, you tell a story where emotions conflict rapidly, from happy to sad and back. Her emotions should be on a rollercoaster: up, down, sideways! A little confusion is good. Intensify the feelings as you go. You can even do this in one sentence, in which you express approval of the woman's perceived weakness or your disapproval of her positive attributes.

Instead of the story, you can also ask her questions, moving back and forth from present to future - even better if you anchor her positive thoughts to you. You can also do this physically, by having her follow you. Move further away each time. Can you fractionate over text? As part of face-to-face enslavement, yes, but it doesn't work on its own. It is good when you don't know her that well and are still in the intrigue/rapport stages. If you're already with her - for example, you're looking to enslave your wife, then you want to deepen the attraction using implanted commands.

You'll need to send two texts to make sure that the command slips by and that she focuses on the second part of the message, which is the part that entices her. The command is implanted into her subconscious through the first one. As always, especially when you're expressing disapproval, you must do it confidently. She needs to chase you, not the other way around.

Black Rose sequence

This is the final step in the IRAE process and the enslavement here is complete. Your target's identity is erased, to be replaced by one that submits to you emotionally. Remember, we're not talking about physical enslavement! This is a form of fractionation, where the rollercoaster ride goes very high and very low. You're using hypnosis to get her so absorbed by the character you've created that her experience with you is emotionally intense. You'll have her feel these highs and lows in her body and she'll be shifting back and forth from pleasure to pain. This induces a trance, during which you can introduce a more submissive identity.

It's easier to get her in the right frame of mind if you tell her to pretend to be hypnotized. The mind has a hard time role-playing, so this will help her slip into the trance you're looking to induce. Giver her positive affirmations (not about her body, but about some other characteristics, so self-doubt doesn't rise up). Then, create a vivid future world with her, making sure you hit all of the senses. If you want to implant sex, for example, you could vividly create a future projection of the two of you in a romantic entanglement. You don't want to be crude or vulgar at this stage. Give her a little twist at the end - "Of course that wouldn't happen!" You can use this to get rid of a boyfriend too - imagine the dream lover whose traits are similar to yours and her current lover will fall well short.

The future projection is key for her to develop that emotional attachment to you and your imagined future together.

Chapter Summary

- Other covert tactics use the power of mind control to have and dominate the woman you want.
- The Shogun method uses a four-step process and sequences within those steps to control the woman you desire.

In the next chapter, we will focus on the secrets of successful female seductresses.

CHAPTER EIGHT:

Seductress Secrets of Seduction

Although men and women want similar things from life, the tricks a seductress uses are a bit different from her male counterparts. As I discussed earlier in the paradox of seduction, both men and women want to be seduced. They want to feel the thrill of attention and experience the charm and enticement used in seduction.

The ambiguities of seduction

Men have long used their physical power and status to dominate women and other men. Yet, it's not only men who take power from others and use it to their advantage. As male seducers tend to be calm and confident, women dress and use make-up seductively to attract a potential mate. Both women and men are at the mercy of their "lizard" brains - the parts that we inherited from our reptilian ancestors. This part of the brain is quite different from our rational, thinking human brains. Seduction appeals to the lizard brain and logic and reason are thrown by the wayside when we're being seduced. This is true for men as well as women. Society is designed to appeal to the rational, human parts of the brain. But, underneath we're animals that yearn to return to the wild!

Introduction to men's psychology

One simple seduction trick that works on almost everyone: find the emotion that most entices your target and provide plenty of it! If you're dating a shrink, they like to feel insightful. So, make them feel that their insights are both welcome and amazing. Men say they value honesty in their partners. If you've had cosmetic procedures, like a boob job or facelift, men wonder if you're being dishonest about other issues, too.

Here's a trick you might not have thought of if you desire an intelligent man: look at his body hair. High intelligence in men is correlated with an abundance of body hair.[18] Not exactly an expected insight!

Although men and women are more alike than they are different, some specific differences relate to how you should approach men you intend to seduce. The part of the brain that makes people territorial is larger in men than in women. That's why they can become violent when they perceive a threat in either their physical or relationship territory. So is the amygdala, which is a part of the lizard brain that is intimately involved in the fight-or-flight response, but also sexual desire.

Finally, the area of the brain that's devoted to sexual pursuit is also much larger in men than it is in women. Boys begin manufacturing gobs of testosterone once they hit their teens - 20 times the amount of their female peers - which means they're hormonally and mentally very interested in sex. It's also why they glaze over at the sight of female breasts - the visual circuits in their brains are constantly searching for fertile partners.[19] This doesn't mean that he's constantly thinking about the pair he just got a good look at. The attention comes and then dissipates. Then, he'll start thinking about other things, like what's for dinner. Don't misunderstand his poker face, though. His emotional

---

[18] https://www.dailymail.co.uk/femail/article-426320/The-psychology-seduction.html
[19] http://edition.cnn.com/2010/OPINION/03/23/brizendine.male.brain/index.html

reactions are as strong and sometimes even stronger than a woman's - he just hides his better.

Maybe because his visual circuits are stronger, men don't need to have a lot of context or relationship in order to be aroused. Mainly, they just need to see the body parts they want to see and they're good to go.[20] That's why dressing seductively and putting on suggestive make-up works so well - men are visual creatures in a way that women are not. Men don't do well with ambiguity in a hierarchy. Their brains prefer a clear chain of command and the military can actually help curb aggressive behavior, simply by reducing this anxiety.[21]

Men are also often happy with a number of sexual partners - novelty is attractive to all brains and men don't have the same social pressure about being slut-shamed. Some of them are very attuned to women who are lonely or lacking something in their lives. They may be upfront about their intentions and will assume that women are looking for sex, too. Having sex can be a transcendent experience.

"It is the ecstasy of wanting and being wanted." - Anonymous

If you're a woman interested in older men, know that they go through a time of life called andropause. If his wife has had kids, his testosterone level dropped while she was pregnant. During andropause, he actually starts manufacturing more estrogen. If his testosterone gets too low, he'll be grouchy and irritable and may need to supplement and get more exercise. He might be a great grandfather if he's got a lot of the bonding hormone oxytocin sloshing around. He could be more affectionate with his grandkids than he ever was with his own. Older men get very lonely after widowhood or divorce and you might just be the right person to get him socializing again.

Women have more mirror neurons, which are the nerves that fire when they reflect on what someone else is doing. They're key to

---

[20] https://www.psychologytoday.com/us/blog/love-and-sex-in-the-digital-age/201506/what-turns-guys-understanding-male-sexual-desire
[21] https://www.livescience.com/14422-10-facts-male-brains.html

empathy, which is why women are often more emotionally attuned to their partners than men. When men spot an attractive potential partner, their brains release dopamine. This occurs whether they're partnered or not. The decision to make a move or not can be disastrous, depending on the circumstances, and yet men continue to do it. Why? Much of it comes down to higher testosterone levels. A man with lower testosterone is more suited to having a family and sticking to it. Research shows that men with higher amounts of testosterone tend to get married less often and when they do marry, they're more likely to cheat and/or get divorced.[22]

Beautiful women cause the man's larger amygdala to fire at approximately the same time that his decision-making center in the prefrontal cortex (part of the rational brain) checks out - not a good time for good decision-making! Strong visual circuits mean that gorgeous girls and porn activate dopamine much more for men than they do for women. Women have better access to the right hemisphere of the brain, which is good and bad for relationships. It tends to be more negative, which is partially why women get depressed more often than men. But they're also good at seeing the overall, big picture, which leads to women dumping men more often than the other way around. They're more negative but can also see when something's not working out faster.

Body language and nonverbal cues

Communication isn't expressed mostly in words, as many of us often think. Over half the message is delivered nonverbally, including gestures, posture, and facial movements. In fact, words are less than 10 percent of communication![23] Many aspects of body language are the same for men as they are for women. Standing up straight with shoulders thrown back exudes confidence - standing with arms crossed denotes defensiveness.

---

[22] https://www.menshealth.com/sex-women/a19516672/understanding-sex-and-the-brain/
[23] https://sexyconfidence.com/how-to-seduce-men-with-body-language/

Signs of seduction include prolonged eye contact. Making eye contact shows interest in the other person. Looking a hint too long and then slowly looking away can be quite erotic. You might also slowly and obviously drop your gaze to his lips. Lick your lips, smile slyly, or use other similar facial expressions. Touching is also very suggestive when done right! And a positive, pleasant tone makes a big difference when you're seducing, compared to a harsh one.

Earlier, you learned about some of the tactics that men use to seduce women. These same cues can work for women trying to seduce men. For example, familiarity breeds interest. They have to notice you before they can be attracted to you. Walking back and forth near your target helps them get used to seeing you. Even bumping into them, especially if you're in a crowded scene, will achieve this goal as well. In addition, movement catches the eye. You might choose to drop something - maybe not your phone, which could break, but your keys or a napkin. This will also attract interest.

Another way to exploit the human brain's desire for novelty is to appear exotic. If you're a different culture or ethnicity, play it up. Emphasize your differences from the standard look. This will help you get noticed in the crowd and also appeal to those who like the exotic. You'll promise adventure just from your looks when you're not boring and/or the norm. Brains also love symmetry, so do your best to look symmetrical. The right clothing can really help with this.

Let them know that you welcome their approach. Particularly if you're shorter than he is, it can be very effective to duck your head a bit and then look up through your eyelashes. It's a bit like a little girl and makes you look innocent. He'll know you won't bite his head off if he starts talking to you!

When you're talking to your target, make a cute move, like lifting one shoulder and cocking your head. It works! Show a little vulnerability, which will particularly appeal to men who have rescuer fantasies. Touch your neck, which is a sign of weakness. Or your wrist, which is another point of weakness. Hold your right wrist with your left hand and you'll look approachable.

Reflect the movements he's making. Do you mirror someone you have no interest in? Of course not. He'll get the message. Use your posture to seduce him, too. When you hold your shoulders back and stand tall, it pushes out the breasts that (many) men love to look at. Give him a genuine smile that reaches your eyes, not the smile of a flight attendant or other service worker. Face him, especially (this is going to sound weird) with your belly button. Even if your head's turned away, most of your body is aimed in his direction, which tells him you're interested. Recall that movement draws attention and play with your hair. Twirl it, toss it back, and slowly put it up while you're in front of him and let his imagination run wild!

Toying with clothes can also be very sensual. Slipping your foot slowly and deliberately in and out of your shoe. Slowly and deliberately cross and recross your legs, playing with the pendant that dangles just above your breasts. Swing your hips. Lean toward him, which signals interest. You also want to stand or sit closer than strangers normally position themselves. Not too close, in the friends and family zone, but not so far that he can't tell you're drawing him in. You can turn your shoulder toward him, put the opposite hand on that shoulder, and lean your cheek on your hand - especially when you're making eye contact the whole time.

Maybe even more importantly, make sure you're wearing clothes and accessories that make YOU feel good! They'll help you feel more confident. Rather than worrying about tugging at your hem or that stupid button that keeps wanting to slide out of the buttonhole, you can focus on when you want to flash your brilliant smile or lick your lips suggestively. You can also stay in the moment of the seduction, doing what comes naturally and feels right that very second. This is the most enjoyable way to be with a man. You can read his reactions and ramp up what gets a positive reaction to lure him in.

Temptress mind games

Now you've mastered the art of using physical cues to mess with your target, it's time to start playing some mind games. Men are supposed to be the calm, rational, logical ones. Being unpredictable and irrational creates a powerful attraction for some men who like to be swept up in an emotional game. You can also stir him up by using mixed feelings, where you alternate between heat and distance. It's confusing, unpredictable, and probably novel for him, too.

Similarly, try mixed signals when you want to, well, mix it up. Push-pull is a good example of this game, but try some variations, too. Assume an angelic appearance but be naughty underneath. If you've got a baby face, wear serious clothes, like a business suit. Or, you can try wearing a white dress to pump up the innocent look, but make the dress and accessories VERY revealing. If you're wearing a business suit and look like you're no-nonsense, act submissive or have very innocent lingerie underneath.

Just as triangulation works with women, a woman can play this game with men. Incite jealousy by drawing him in, then flirting with another man. Get him emotionally hot and bothered.

Women are supposed to be either a Madonna or a whore, so...play both! He'll appreciate the confusion and not knowing which way is up and he'll love the tumble into bed. While you're making out, enjoy the lust and the pleasure sensations. Then stop and resist for a bit. This also plays into the unpredictability that men enjoy. You'll probably find that you enjoy it, too! You're lost in the urge...but then you have to fight your desire...which you'll eventually succumb to anyway. But he doesn't know that and you'll create some real suspense for him. Short bursts of extreme sexual action combined with withdrawal will leave him both dazed and dying for more. Whirlwind sexual passion is exactly what he wants and he wants more of it. So, of course, you can't give it to him again right away - that's just too boring and predictable. Egg him on in weird places, like waiting in line at the store, where you can brush his crotch. When you're dining with parents, give him a little footsie action.

Be dangerous - remember he's supposed to be logical, so a touch of craziness might just be what the seduction doctor ordered. Not full-on crazy, though! Enough that it's novel and unpredictable. Conversely, some men really dig a maternal act, so let a little regression creep in. Tuck him under the covers, kiss him on the forehead. This is a great way to hook a Player. Or, invert the regression so you're acting more youthful. Men love to revisit their youth, particularly older men who can be fatherly and still get sex, for them, this is a potent combo. Sugar daddies in particular fall for this one pretty easily. Don't be too much of a baby though, that's off-putting.

Use your words. It's true body language is more important in communication, but why not let your words really count? Don't be too vulgar or crude or swear: you still want to demonstrate that you're a high-quality woman. But you can be incredibly suggestive with your words, while using some of the body language techniques described in the last section. Touching and poking below the belt also works very well. You might "accidentally" brush against his chest or crotch, or brush him *with* your breasts or crotch. You can be more obvious about his crotch too, which deliberately asks him if he's man enough to come for you. He is. And if not, you're not interested anyway, are you?

If he's cheated or otherwise hurt you, guilt-trip him. Let him know how much he hurt you. This won't work with a narcissist, who doesn't care if he hurt you, or a sociopath, where the cruelty is the point.

Speaking of cruelty, you need to be careful with this last mind game. Violence and emotional abuse are not something you want to inflict on people. Having said that, sexual aggressiveness, violence, and attraction can be incredibly powerful when combined. Sex during a fight can be absolutely amazing and aggressiveness plus sex, dominating your man, will appeal to any latent masochistic tendencies he might have.

Triggering emotional attraction in men

In earlier chapters, I mentioned that seduction is a game of emotions. Although men believe themselves to be logical and rational, they can be swept away with emotions just as women can. In fact, you need him to set aside his thinking brain in order for him to be seduced. The human brain loves patterns and it loves recognizing patterns. The trick is to know which patterns unlock the emotions in men because some are different from the ones that work on women.

People feel good when they're making progress toward a goal. Often, the little gains end up being more pleasurable than the goal itself! That's why standard goal-setting suggests you should identify your big goals, but then make smaller ones so you can see progress as you go. With men, playing hard to get taps into this instinct for the chase and tiny achievements toward the ultimate goal of sex.

Imagine one little girl fleeing from a war-torn country - there's a point to this, I promise - with her little backpack, not knowing where she's going. You feel empathy for her plight, don't you? You want to help her. But when you imagine millions of people fleeing this country, not knowing where they're going, with only the worldly possessions they can carry, it's harder to empathize. In research, this is called compassion collapse and it happens because the human ability to empathize decreases when there's no meaningful way to help. This is why nonprofits will often feature one specific child or family in their calls for donations[24]. Men are naturally less empathetic than women in the first place. They want to make their woman happy, but that goal is too vague and they don't really know how to go about it. Unless you give them particular ways to make you happy and trigger his empathy, they'll drift off into not caring about you. Men like missions, so give him one. It doesn't have to be finding the Holy Grail, but something he can easily picture in his mind.

---

[24] https://commitmentconnection.com/the-secret-to-understanding-what-triggers-attraction-in-men/

People's natural instinct is to do favors for others. We've been socialized to give and that's often what women do when trying to lure a particular man to them. But that's not the right way to truly develop a bond. Instead, ask him for a favor. Research shows that the human brain is more activated when giving a gift than when receiving it.[25] So ask him to give you something. It doesn't have to be an actual present - advice is better. Ask him for his help on a problem you're having at work, or maybe he can find out what new tires you should put on your car!

Men want relationships that fit who they are, in the way that they want to see themselves. If a man wants to see himself as a hero, he'll bond to the woman who allows him to be that hero. He needs to enjoy who he is when he's with you. Most men want to be the hero. That's how they've been socialized. Bond with him by telling him a story that reveals some needs of your own and helps him meet those needs. Now it feels right for him to be with you because you're feeding that need he has.

In addition to helping him be the version of himself that he's always wanted, there are ways to be emotionally attractive to men.

Be patient

We all fumble through this life having lost the instruction manual! Men like women who don't demand everything be done the right way the first time all the time. They also like someone who asks what they meant first before taking offense because they didn't phrase it correctly. Remember, women have the upper hand in the language aspects of the brain.

Be a good listener

Contrary to popular opinion, men do like to talk. But it can be hard for them to have serious discussions. Let them express their full thought before jumping to conclusions.

---

[25] https://www.huffpost.com/entry/how-to-scientifically-trigger-his-emotional-desire_b_59bab8b4e4b06b71800c3781

Be self-confident

Don't spend too much time talking about your flaws, especially the physical ones. Let him see you as self-assured. That takes the burden off him to fulfill this need.

Be in the moment

Leave the past in the past. No one really enjoys listening to memories dredged up about bad ex-boyfriends...or even good ones! Enjoy the relationship you have in front of you. This tactic also helps him feel less insecure compared to your previous relationships.

Focus on the positive

Who likes a Debbie Downer? Not men, anyway. Give their ideas some time to ripen before you start criticizing or pointing out flaws.

Communicate honestly and openly

If there's a problem, let him know so he can fix it. Recall that men have less empathy than women, so they're going to be even worse at reading minds. He can't do it, so don't make him. Ask him about things to make sure that you understand his intentions, instead of assuming that you know what's going on in his head.

Be a secret-keeper

In a strong relationship, you'll be opening up to each other and revealing secrets that many other people don't know about you. Keep the secrets he tells you like you're a lockbox. No one in your family needs to know his vulnerabilities and weaknesses and don't throw them back in his face during an argument.

Appreciate the effort made

None of us are perfect. Building on patience, men like it when you also see that they've made a genuine effort (when they've made one, of course). They probably didn't get it right on the first try, but they tried, and they love it when you acknowledge that.

Hot buttons for the hero instinct

Now you know how important it is to make a man feel like a hero when you want some kind of relationship with him. If you're genuinely in distress, this might be pretty easy. But what if you're not? Fortunately, there are some methods to use to trigger it without a crisis in your own life. Even if you're a strong, independent woman, use his hero instinct to bond him with you.

We already discussed asking him for help or advice. Even little everyday things will trigger his desire to be a hero. You might already be an expert on fixing cars and toilets. So what? Let him lift a finger to help you. If you're having difficulty opening up a jar, ask him to do it. It's a tiny thing, but when you show you appreciate it, he will feel like the hero he wants to be.

Letting him be a man, with male hobbies and male decor, is also greatly appreciated. Men like the fact that you're feminine, but they don't necessarily want to be feminine themselves. If his place is messy, well, who cares. You're just enjoying spending time with him. If you don't like the sports he watches, don't make him watch the Hallmark Mysteries & Movies channel with you instead.

Just like women, men don't like it when things come too easily. They like a bit of a challenge, which is another reason playing hard to get works so well with them. You can find other challenges for him and ways to earn your respect. Don't give it automatically - let him work for it. Have your man win you over by succeeding in the challenge you set for him.

The language of male desire

Emotional triggers are different for men and women and so is the language that gets you all hot and bothered. Make sure he's hearing the words that work for him, too. Some of them may seem a little silly to you, but you're triggering his affection for you so that you can bond more deeply - in language that works with the male brain. Tell him that you're his. This offers the loyalty he craves. You might also say you want only him, which will ease his anxiety about coming on too strong. Assure him that you're in it together, which will soothe any financial worries he might have.

As we've discussed, men are visual creatures and appealing to some of his physical characteristics in a way that makes him more secure will provide great rewards. You might ask him if it's getting bigger, which helps him put to rest all his insecurities about size. (And most men have this insecurity, even if they don't show it right away.) Or the perennial, "Have you been working out?" Women go to the gym, but men workout, so you're flattering his masculinity while soothing any physical appearance issues he might have. When you want to trigger that hero instinct, let him know he makes you feel safe.

Appreciate the things he does for you while showing your vulnerability. "When I met you I wasn't sure I deserved you, but you always know the right thing to say when I'm feeling down." Let him know that he excites you even when doing more mundane things, like hugging. This gives him the idea that underneath, you are always thinking and fantasizing about him.

And don't forget to tell him you love him!

Chapter Summary

- Men's brains are more visually oriented and bathed in testosterone, so they have different triggers, including the thrill of the chase and the visual pleasure of lingerie.
- Body language and nonverbal cues work very well on visually-oriented men to draw attention to yourself and deepen the attraction.
- Different mind games and emotional triggers, as well as different language, will bond men to you for as long as you wish.
- This is especially true when you trigger his hero instinct and allow him to be your hero, even in little ways.

In the next chapter, you will learn how to use seduction techniques outside a romantic or sexual relationship.

CHAPTER NINE:

Applied Seduction

So far, most of our discussion has been about romantic or sexual seduction. But seducing others at work, or even in your everyday life, can bring you great rewards. Obviously, you're going to approach your supervisor or other colleagues in a completely different way! But you can use some of the same techniques in a different way, with the same ultimate goal: to get what you want from other people.

Seduce your (nonsexual) way to a career boost

Let what you've learned about romantic seduction unlock the potential for more career opportunities.

Use a creative approach to get past the gatekeepers

You know you could get the business - or the job - if you could just get in to see the right people. But they're usually very busy and they've hired people to keep them from being bothered by every vendor or every job applicant. The gatekeepers could be the receptionist, the personal assistant, or even HR. They've heard the same opening lines a million times and they're tired of it. They'll shoot you down before you even have a chance.

If you hit them with something they weren't expecting, you can slide right past them before they even know what hit them. Even an interesting or creative story could work.

On LinkedIn, a social platform mostly for the business-to-business (B2B) crowd, I saw a post that talked about how a job applicant entered an office acting like a delivery guy and delivered a box of doughnuts along with their resume. They got right through the gatekeepers!

Don't be boring

The human brain's love for novelty isn't just for sexual partners. Our brains love anything new. Just as you can't bore a potential lover to death because they'll just take off, you can't bore a potential business partner to death either. Talk about something different. Do something different in the interview to get them to engage with you. Be fun and interesting, just as you would with a new seduction target.

Show social proof

Just as I recommended that you hit the club with tons of attractive people to show your magnetism, companies love to see that you've worked with other well-known companies. If you could make it there, you could make it anywhere: the Sinatra test.[26] For freelancers and consultants, social proof often shows up as testimonials or case studies.

You're the prize, so use some swagger

People like to see confidence and that doesn't change just because you're in the boardroom instead of the bedroom. Being needy and desperate turns off members of both sexes, whether you're trying to sell a product or yourself as the company's new hire. When you interview, have the attitude that you're also interviewing them to make sure it's the

---

[26] https://www.news.com.au/finance/work/seduction-tactics-to-boost-your-career/news-story/6fce129b118a03dfde4b68c4169ababf

right fit for you. Act like you've got so many companies chasing you, you can choose who you work with.

Just as when finding a new romantic partner, being chased by plenty of others may or may not be true. But it's good practice to act as if it is. Bring on that swagger. Don't tell them only what they want to hear or try too hard. That's a major turn-off!

Don't fall for their tests

Similarly, prospects, clients, and interviewers may push you to see how far they can go. They may lowball you on price or fees. If what they're offering doesn't work for you, make sure they know it. Don't be so desperate for the business that you're willing to incur a loss to work with them.

Be attractive so they come to you

You're cool, calm, and collected, luring them in rather than chasing them. Sound familiar? You also don't want to lower your price (see above) because the cost isn't what drives people to buy. If you drop your price, you're not more attractive, you're just less profitable.

"Be the flame, not the moth." - Casanova

Don't chase your customers or sales. Be so attractive that you're the flame and customers (or hiring managers) come to you instead.

Keep flirting after you close the deal

Continue to nurture your clients even after they've made the purchase. This will help you increase follow-on sales, as well as referrals. Keep the relationship going and you'll be a sales all-star instead of having to chase after the sale. Word of warning, however: acting distant is not going to lure in your clients the way it lures in romantic partners!

Seduction in business, marketing, and sales

Give your (business) targets enough information about you and/or your business or product to tantalize them. Awaken their curiosity and playfulness, just as you would do for a romantic target. Use whatever kind of social charm you've got. For example, some people are witty, others are cute. Some play on their intelligence. Whatever comes naturally to you, use it.

People don't like to be sold to, so the trick is to sell them without selling them! This sounds hard, but the tactics of seduction help you do this. You can create events that don't seem like marketing tactics, though of course, they are. Even though men are more visually-oriented than women, pretty much all humans are visual. Make sure your marketing contains enough pictures to get your point across. I discussed in earlier chapters the fact that seduction is about filling a need, or a lack, that someone has. It works exactly the same way in sales. You develop a connection with your prospects and clients so that you understand what their needs are.

Most clients don't really need the widget or gadget or whatever service you're selling. What they need is validation from their supervisor. A way to get their jobs done faster, not for the sake of the job, but so they can go home earlier and spend time with their families. They're looking for a way to save money so they can allocate more budget to other projects, or look good in front of their superiors.

Another way to look at it is that customers like something to aspire to. Your product helps them be a better version of themselves. You just have to figure out what version they're looking for and target that. If you're a writer, your prospects don't need your words so much. They need someone else to take care of something that bewilders them or frees up time for them to work on their business. Selling vacuums? Your prospect doesn't need a robot vacuum that has a 3-liter capacity. They need to find more time they can spend with their families. As you develop your relationship, you uncover these needs and then you position yourself as the perfect person with the perfect product or service to take care of this need. People don't buy based on logic and reason. They buy based on emotion, which is the basis of seduction, too.

Build emotional connections with your targets. You can ask them questions that skew them towards you and your product, as long as you ask in the right away. You can also prep the environment with music, scent, and visual appeal in order to sway them.

Remember that it takes time to build these relationships. When you go to the club, most of the time you can't jump directly from approaching a potential lover to having sex with them in a brief period of time. You need to let the attraction and comfort develop before you start closing the deal. Likewise, if you jump right from introducing yourself to a hard sell, your prospect will be turned off. Take the time to build the connection first instead of scaring them off. Sometimes it's just not going to work. The sale isn't going to happen. As long as you detach yourself from the results, you'll be fine. You're freed up to go attract the next prospect. If you are too attached to the outcome, every rejection is crushing.

When you're selling with seduction, you end up doing less work. You're not chasing down as many leads, but working with well-qualified ones who want to do business with you. Seducing your prospects can be more fun because it's about skill instead of brute-force numbers. Digital content is the bait you drop. Once you've created it you can dunk in lots of different pools to see which ones rise to it more often, without much more work on your part. Let the prospects qualify themselves and come to you. You can help them qualify themselves by letting them feel like they're a member of some elite club. Your product is not for everyone. In fact, it might be too powerful for some!

Shut off the phone when you're with your self-qualified prospects. Or any prospects, for that matter. Watching someone get distracted by their phone is a business boner-killer, too. Listen to what they have to say. Everyone likes undivided attention! Make it about them, not you (or your quota). Enjoy the journey. If you're using the seductive methods correctly, you'll probably find the seduction is better than the close! This works best if you genuinely believe in the product or service that you're selling. If you don't, it's very hard to get into the mindset that you're doing your prospects and clients a favor by giving them the opportunity to purchase. Visualize your success as part of having the right mindset.

See yourself overcoming objections, without coming across as desperate. Picture yourself in conversation and getting the information that you need to know to solve their problem. The mind can't tell the difference between a real scene and an imaginary one, so give it successful scenes. Make sure your visualization includes emotions and other senses too, so that you're having a complete experience. You can also visualize what life is like for your prospects, by stepping into their shoes and seeing the world from their perspective instead of yours. When you're selling, provide a rich fantasy for your clients as to what their life looks like when you've solved their problem. Shift their focus on to you with grabby headlines, or some drama. Confuse them and use plenty of humor, as long as you're not acting goofy.

Your clients and prospects need to have the right frame of mind and be ready to buy when you actually start selling. You can help this process along by taking them on a mental journey, usually with a story, that makes them think they do have a need for whatever you're selling.

You're in charge and you display that with your self-assurance, without being a bully or ordering people around. As noted before, people like to be led. Be the leader that gets them to believe it's their idea to buy, not yours! You can also use the "guru phenomenon" to increase sales. Sometimes a product doesn't take off until a guru, influencer, or expert has signed off on it. If you don't have a guru handy, you can just quote an authority figure in the field. Let the prospect's imagination take off from there. Want to improve even more on that idea? You, too, can become a guru, or expert on the subject. Position yourself that you have the edge on whatever your clients are looking for. Help them shift their perception of you. You can add in tips and advice to your sales copy.

When you're negotiating, you want to appear a little mysterious. Like you have a card you haven't played...because you don't need to.

You're not desperate for a good outcome, because you're too confident for that. Your negotiation partner has to come to you and impress upon you how good their solution is for you. Again, this should sound pretty familiar to you by now!

To be clear, you're not trying to use or manipulate the other side. You're just confident and empowered, which makes you seductive in business. Don't make yourself too available, or rush to let prospects know everything about you. Maintaining a little bit of an air of exclusivity is attractive. Do you want to pitch someone in the media? Maybe you're looking for more eyes on your product or service. Here's another good place to practice your seduction techniques. Journalists are people, too! Nail your intro and don't make it too long. Be concise enough that your message is clear. Would you send out a mass email to all the people you know when you're searching for a date? That would never work, and it doesn't work on media contacts either. Send personalized messages, tailored to your target. Make sure that you're aiming at the right target. If your message is about consumer products, don't send it to the reporter who covers the foreign news beat.

Follow up and not in a creepy way. Sometimes emails get buried or the journalists themselves are buried under mountains of work. If you don't hear back, try them again. But don't stand outside their (online) door with your finger on the doorbell either.

Once your target has succumbed...keep flirting! Nurture the relationship, just as you do with other business contacts.

All this can be broken down into three major categories. When you're using seductive selling and marketing, you:

1. Entice them

Your creativity, humor, and confidence are all designed to make prospects and clients come to you. To chase you and your product. To feel that it's designed just for them and their needs.

2. Enrich them

Create a lasting bond with them by connecting, listening, and discovering what their needs are.

3. Enable them

Let them imagine what a comfortable and less costly life they'll lead with you guiding them! Painting the rich fantasy future seduces them into believing that you're the answer.

Everyday seduction

By being able to charm people, you can entice them into giving you what you want. As long as it's in their power to do so! There are plenty of arenas outside business and bed where a little seduction goes a long way.

Desire

First, you have to be clear about what it is you want. When you don't know, you can't figure out the steps to get there, much less entice anyone into giving something to you! They must understand what you're asking for in order to provide it. Suppose you go out to the club, but you're not entirely sure why you're there. Is it to have fun with your friends? Find a man to have sex with? Find a woman to start a relationship with? Depending on your goal for the evening, you'll do things very differently. You don't approach friends the same way you open up to a potential lover.

Once you've figured out what you want, you'll know what language to use and what you need to ask for or allow people to give you. You'll go into a situation knowing what you need to do in order to get what you desire.

Self-confidence

By now you've recognized that seduction has a lot to do with leading other people. You may not always want to make it clear that you're the one in charge because some people need to believe that they're the ones in charge. This doesn't bother you...because you know they're wrong! In order to be led, however, people need to believe in the leader. If they don't, they will simply refuse to follow. Which means you need to act and speak like the leader you are. This is much easier when you radiate self-assurance. It's an invitation to the people who want to follow because it signals to them that here's someone who knows what they're doing! This is especially true for men, who need clear social hierarchies to feel comfortable.

Non-verbal communication

The body tells most of the story, so make sure that you know how to use it. Even when you're not feeling particularly confident, you can stand in confident poses. When it comes to confidence, "fake it 'til you make it" actually works. Stand up straight with shoulders back, this is a confident pose, as is standing with your legs spread wide, taking up the room that you deserve. Hold your head high and make direct eye contact. It's people without self-confidence that look at their feet, the door, anywhere but the face of the person they're speaking with.

You can also express what you want and don't want without using words. Using your arms crossed in front of you as a shield, leaning away from someone who's in your space, and other similar poses let people know they're not welcome. By the same token, making eye contact, smiling, and putting your phone away, all signal positive intentions toward your target.

Arousal

In order to do as you'd like, your target needs to feel an emotional pull towards you, strong enough to push past any kind of inertia. Once you've discovered their need and lured it out of them, they'll want to do as you wish. Seduction is a way to understand what the other person wants. It's only after you've satisfied their emotional need, whatever it is, that you can entice them to do what you want them to do.

Chapter Summary

- Seduction isn't just for sex.
- Similar seductive methods taught earlier can help you boost your career without sex.
- Business, marketing, and sales are all more effective when you use seductive techniques, such as discovering their emotional needs and filling them.
- There are many times in daily life when seducing other people gets you what you want.

In the next chapter, you will learn about using seduction to find your way through life.

CHAPTER TEN:

Using Principles of Seduction to Navigate Through Life

Now you have a good understanding of seduction and how to use it to find business and romantic partners. But you can also use it to forge a path through life. You don't have to be manipulative or deceitful, but you can be seductive. You can think of seduction as basically communication, leadership, or leveraging your knowledge of human nature.

The lost art of seduction

Another way to look at seduction is that it's based on surprise. The novelty our brains crave is sated by someone who keeps surprising us. This is how you hook a romantic partner for life: you continually surprise them. It's when people get bored or feel that they're in a rut that the thought of cheating is likely to rear its ugly head. But if your partner doesn't know what's going to happen next? They'll stick around just to find out!

You can't use the element of surprise all the time, but often enough to spice things up. It works very well too when you're starting to lure in your target. They'll love the fact that you're spontaneous and unpredictable. Boring is not attractive, or enticing, or alluring. The more you can spice things up and change them around, the more they'll be thinking about you. It's also the habit of getting into someone's head. We've lost that ability, as we spend more and more time in front of screens and passively accepting the entertainment that some company's algorithm provides. In order to seduce someone, you must observe them closely. Notice the details that give them away. Find the soft spot underneath your target's exterior.

Whether you're looking for a customer or a lover, you'll see the best rewards when you're able to uncover their emotional needs. Remember that seduction is about emotion and that doesn't change whether you're selling a vacuum or yourself as a sexual partner. What needs does your target have that are unmet? You'll need to pay attention to what they say (and don't say) and ask them questions. See how they respond to different stories. Your phone isn't going to tell you that and neither is your video game or social media feed or laptop screen. The only person who can tell you about your target is your target themselves. They might spill it out all upfront, or you might need to tease and entice it out of them.

Power in seduction

In civilized society, we don't usually demonstrate (or take) power by physical force. We have to do it indirectly, which often involves deception. People are pretty gullible when it comes to appearances. This is why acting as if you're confident works so well. You seem like you're confident and so people believe you are.

Mastery

To master something, there are a couple of major requirements. One is that you practice the thing consistently over time. You're always working on it and always trying to improve. The second requirement is that you love it! There's no way you're going to be able to put in the hours over time if you don't love it. There's a lot of repetition, especially of the basics when you're first beginning. You have to learn all the rules and processes. Usually, you're starting on the bottom floor, working your way up as you go. None of this is sustainable or even bearable if you don't love it. You may already have a pretty good idea of what you love. But what if you don't? You have to try lots of things, in that case, to find something. Don't get discouraged if it doesn't happen right away. You might need to expand your search parameters if you keep trying things with no results.

Once you find it, you'll need to make sure you're learning and acquiring skills to go with it. Centuries ago, in Europe (and still today in some European countries), you'd apprentice yourself to an existing master and have them teach you the ropes. These days, the apprenticeship could be in the form of a job. When you're trying to master something, you may not want to take the job with the highest salary on offer. Apprenticeships were usually pretty menial, at least to start. You want to find the job that will promote the most learning for you. Back then, they also didn't have the distractions of the internet, as we do. You'll never master anything if you spend your time on the internet. Just as you need to put the phone down to focus on your target in seduction, put it down when you're trying to master a skill. You need to practice it yourself, not watch endless videos about it or fall down the rabbit hole with tangential topics.

Learning mastery is also learning to avoid or tune out distractions. Once you have the basics down or finished your apprenticeship, you've got to test and experiment. What techniques work for you and which don't? Can you bring any other life experience to shed light on the problem? In other words, you've got to challenge yourself to stay in mastery. If you allow yourself to stop learning and stagnate, you'll lose your grip. Learn the rules so you can break them and find out which ones should stay broken.

Benefits of learning how to seduce

One major advantage of learning how to seduce is that those who do can also learn how to detach from the outcome. The game doesn't work every time. More importantly, when you're so attached to the results,

97

you'll often come across as desperate and needy. But when you can let go of the outcome and focus on the process, you'll be calm and cool without even having to think about it. If you don't get the result you wanted, you'll just try again at another time. You've learned to deal with rejection. Some people never get it and they're crushed every time! But you know it happens and you know that you can bounce right back up. You don't spend a lot of time anticipating it because you know you'll get rejected some of the time. Big deal. Just move on to the next target and don't take it personally. When you know it's just part of the game, it's easier to handle.

Most people who have mastered seduction also end up with fewer regrets because at least they tried! They don't subject themselves to a lot of "if only" and "I wish I'd approached that person" because they went ahead and gave it a shot.

"You miss 100% of the shots you don't take." - Wayne Gretzky

Recent research has shown that when people are on their deathbeds, they don't tend to regret what they actually did. Their regrets are for what they didn't do: like spend more time with other people. If you're out there on a regular basis talking to other people, you won't regret it later. Will you have bad days? Yes. Will there be days full of rejection? Yes. But that doesn't mean that overall you'll do worse than if you'd never been out there. You've learned about how important a positive mindset is. When the negative thoughts come, you just shake them off. Otherwise, you'll be spending too much time in your head instead of out there approaching and opening.

When you come across someone you want to seduce, or even just make them feel important for whatever reason, you know how to listen actively. By now, you're observing details and trying to understand what's going on in the other person's head. You're not listening just to find out when the person will stop speaking so you can jump in with your opinion! Engaging in a conversation can bring you unexpected dividends. There are some days when you just don't want to go out. Maybe a rejection really did sting or you're kind of tired or whatever.

You also know that you need to get out there and practice consistently, so you make sure you go out, even when you're not feeling it. Showing up is half the battle! You've now trained yourself to get out there, whether or not you particularly want to. You can say that you're disciplined and consistent as a result of this practice. Rather than feeling sorry for yourself, you get up and go. It's hard to stay depressed and blue when you're out having an exciting time!

Get what you want in life with these key principles of seduction

You may not call yourself a pick-up artist, but you've got some serious seduction techniques under your belt at this point. Seduction isn't a hobby, though. It's not just about learning how to have sex with someone you really want to have sex with or to get the job you want. It's a fundamental life skill that you need to have in your toolbox. Seduction helps you find happiness because you're able to go out into the world and choose your romantic partner, friends, and other people to be around who support you. Choosing who you spend time with means that you don't settle for whoever happens to be around you, but someone who is truly compatible with you. Don't let doubts and self-limiting beliefs hold you back from getting what you want, or putting these principles and techniques into daily practice in your life. Social seduction skills are learned; just as other skills are. And just like other skills, the more you practice, the more you improve!

The key to navigating your way through the world is that you're much more likely to get what you want when people like you. Being likable is crucial, or else you'll find life very difficult. Fortunately, you can use the principles of seduction to get people to like you, even if you don't necessarily want to lure them to bed or sell them something. Just going out to a restaurant can be better when the wait staff likes you! It's still about finding that unmet need in the other person and filling it in a way they've never experienced before. Are you unhappy because you feel like the world isn't giving you what you want? Perhaps a pay raise, a date, love, companionship? Turns out you need to give to the world before it gives to you.

"Life is a seduction." - Raj Persaud

Instead of being focused on your own unmet needs, find out about someone else's, especially their key frustrations. Use small talk in a specific way to find out what drives the other person and what they need. Once you've given to the world in the form of meeting the needs of one person, you'll find that the world starts giving back - the partner you want, the friends you want. It's also important to remember that there isn't one way to be seductive. Whatever your natural strengths might be - wit, humor, intelligence - use them to charm others into getting what you want. It's not necessarily about being gorgeous. You can be, sure, but you don't have to be to seduce other people. Have you ever seen someone who seems to have eager admirers at their feet wherever they go, but they're not even good looking? They've learned the skills of seduction, so they don't need to be good-looking. One interesting experiment showed how seduction works. Groups of students were sent on dates. One group was told to agree with everything the date said. One was told to disagree with everything. The third group was told to disagree with everything during the first half of the date and then agree with everything in the second half. Afterward, the dates rated how attractive they found the students.

As you might expect, the first group was moderately attractive and the second group was rated as hideous! But the third group was found most attractive of all. Having read the previous parts of this book, this might not surprise you at all. The dates thought the third-group students needed a little time to warm up to them and that they had warmed the students up. In other words, that they had done the seducing. Casanova (reportedly) found an attractive actress in a bar who had a lisp and couldn't pronounce her Rs properly. Did he offer to send her to elocution lessons? Did he tell her to go see someone he knew who had experience with the problem and could work with her? No. He went home and wrote a play that had no Rs in it. Once complete, he returned to the bar and presented it to her. Seduction complete! This was probably the first time anyone had actually written a play for her, much less one that was tailored to the issue that she had. He didn't tell her that she needed fixing or that he was interested in her. She had to get her problem fixed first. So, he wrote the play.

How many times do we inadvertently indicate that the other person needs fixing? We'd probably think we were helping the actress if we offered her elocution lessons. But the play was sexy. Its message of, "Don't change a thing! You are perfect the way you are!" is incredibly sexy. And, of course, she was seduced by it. She didn't really need elocution lessons. She needed a play that wouldn't feature her speech impediment. That's the need that Casanova met, in a way no one ever had before.

You can think of relationships as having three phases: attraction, interest, and maintenance. In a long-term relationship, you'll continue that cycle many times, or else interest can fall off a cliff or people get bored. This is true for romantic or sexual relationships. But it's also true for many other relationships you have in your life: with customers, with friends, and many others. Take these principles and psychological techniques and use them to improve your life. Is it a game? Maybe. But others are certainly playing it, so you're going to have a hard time if you refuse. Give before you expect to receive - that's the way it works best for you to ultimately achieve your goals and get what you want in life.

Chapter Summary

- Seduction is almost a lost art because not enough people pay attention to the human being in front of them, being distracted with their own needs and electronic gadgets.
- You need to be able to seduce people to get what you want, including power.
- Mastery of seduction requires time and persistent practice and there are side benefits to this practice, as well.
- Seduction is a life skill you need to learn to survive, not just a hobby or way to have more sex.

CONCLUSION

Seduction is both an art and a science. It builds on fundamental knowledge that we have about how the human brain works, including the differences between male and female brains. This is important when we talk about sexual seduction! But it's also an art, in regards to how you use verbal and nonverbal communication to attract your targets and lure them in. Although in recent years, "pick-up artist" (PUA) groups have become known for their attempts to teach men how to pick up women, in reality, seduction communities have been around for a long time. Some are fortunate enough to be mentored by someone who knows how to play the game, but not all are.

Seduction has been popularly thought of to be the province of people who are strong in one or more characteristics of what's known as the Dark Triad: narcissism, Machiavellianism, and psychopathy. Research actually shows that people who are moderate in one or more of these traits can actually be very successful in business and other aspects of life. There's a lot of debate about whether seduction is moral. Certainly, to those who think of seduction as a game for men to have sex with women and then leave them, it looks immoral, or unethical, at the least. But popular stereotypes don't tell the whole story. A seducer gets to know their target so that they can identify their unmet need. This may mean that their target is showered with attention, which they might not be getting enough of elsewhere. A key technique in seduction is getting into another person's head and seeing the world as they do - stepping into their shoes. Granted, this is with the ultimate goal of getting what the seducer wants. But, it still doesn't sound very narcissistic, does it? Learning what makes the other person tick and surprising them with little gifts (not necessarily monetary) is another seduction technique that benefits the other person, too.

For those who may still think seduction is immoral, consider that it's an important skill for everyone to learn. To get what you want from the world, first, you need to give. Find the other person's unmet need and then fulfill it in a way they've never seen before. You also need to be likable to attract the right people to you. You can learn to seduce others into liking you.

Knowing what you want from the world helps you to choose partners: romantic, business, or even just friends who bring out the best in you and support you. When you don't learn the skills of seduction, you'll end up with whoever's near you and they may or may not be the most compatible. It's not about having a hobby, it's about survival. To lead the life you want to lead, you'll need to seduce other people in one way or another. Seduction is different from manipulation, where your intentions are concealed from the target. For example, men sometimes manipulate women into bed by having them believe they're interested in a romantic relationship when all they want is sex. Both sexes can seduce, however - it's not limited to just one gender.

Some seduction techniques are different depending on whether you're seducing a man or a woman. Men place more emphasis on the visual and they can reliably be enticed to do a woman's bidding if she triggers his hero instinct. Women often respond well to fantasies that are rich in detail, as well as witty wordplay.

There are plenty of seducer archetypes - the Rake, the Siren, the Coquette. There are also plenty of victims out there! These are sometimes those who have an unmet need, whose reality is so dull that anyone even slightly interesting is like a breath of fresh air. Anyone feeling like they're in a rut, in any kind of way, is a target for seducing. Many seduction techniques are universal, not restricted to one gender or one type of target. They may not only be used to entice a sexual prospect, but business and sales, as well. Human beings love novelty, so surprises or doing something different will usually get the attention you want. We also have unmet needs and a person who promises to fulfill those needs will be very well received. Most people want to be led, so it's crucial for the seducer to be confident and self-assured, not thrown by any tests or disagreements their targets might try to raise as an obstacle.

Humans tend to like a bit of a challenge. We don't necessarily want everything handed to us on a silver platter. A very effective technique, whether you're seducing a sexual target or a prospective client, is to let them come to you. Naturally, you'll need them to be attracted and interested in you and/or your product for this to work, but you don't want to chase them down. Needy and desperate is a turn-off, so create a little distance. You know how great you are (or at least you're projecting it to them), so eventually, they'll come to you. Seduction is not logical and it also may not have anything to do with how physically attractive you are. Most people have a strength that they can use to charm others. For some, it is being beautiful or handsome, but for others, it might be wit or humor. If you've ever seen someone with tons of rabid fans who isn't conventionally attractive, they're using some other strength that comes naturally to them.

You don't have to sleep your way to the top, though you can certainly seduce your way there! If you're a salesperson, you want your prospect hungry for your product. When they believe that they need it and that it's the answer to all their problems, you don't even have to sell them. Remember not to be too available! You'll stir up that need, show them that you're the one who can meet that need, and let them rush to you instead of the other way around.

When you're in business, no matter how you feel about the PUA community, one thing that they teach is very important. Seduction is a process: attraction - comfort - seduction, and trying to adopt these phases out of order results in failure. You won't get customers dying to work with you (or women to sleep with you) if you don't attract them first. You can't seduce them until they've built a comfort level with you. You can end up doing less work because you're making fewer cold calls and allowing the prospects to qualify themselves. There are a number of ways to do this, but it's important that the phases be respected, in business and in bed. If you're trying to sell the instant you meet people, it's not going to work and will lead only to frustration. You need to put in some time with them first before you start trying to close the deal. Time is important in seduction. Not just taking what's needed for the process, but also recognizing that it will take time for you to master these skills. You need to practice them on a consistent basis in order to reach mastery. If you're working on seducing women, you need to talk to one a day or work on your game every day. If you're working on seducing someone in business, you need to be in contact on a regular basis so you can figure out that need and keep flirting after you close it.

I promised to teach you what you need to know about seduction - what it is, how it's been used, and how people currently use it. I've also given you techniques that you can learn and use in real life to get what you want and that's really what seduction is all about. If there's only one thing you take away from this book, it should be this: seduction is a necessary skill that you can learn if you practice consistently. Some people are born knowing how to entice and allure, but many of us aren't. Fortunately, it's something you can learn. If you work on it on a regular basis, you'll improve. It doesn't matter what you look like or how much money you have, as long as you learn and use these methods of seduction.

RESOURCES

About-Secrets. (2013, June 30). Seduction marketing. Retrieved February 19, 2020, from https://www.slideshare.net/mfr786/seduction-marketing

Acton, F. (2020, January 6). Fractionation Texting. Retrieved February 17, 2020, from https://fractionation.net/fractionation-texting/

A-hole Game: Day 1. (2009, January 12). Retrieved February 16, 2020, from https://web.archive.org/web/20140711073602/http:/heartiste.wordpress.com/2009/01/12/a-hole-game-day-1/

Amante, C. (n.d.-a). How to Use Social Proof to Get Girls | Girls Chase. Retrieved February 17, 2020, from https://www.girlschase.com/content/how-use-social-proof-get-girls

Amante, C. (n.d.-b). Tactics Tuesdays: Deconstructing the PUA Neg | Girls Chase. Retrieved February 17, 2020, from https://www.girlschase.com/content/tactics-tuesdays-deconstructing-pua-neg

Anonymous. (2004, June 27). Some of my best friends are women. Retrieved February 18, 2020, from https://www.theguardian.com/world/2004/jun/27/gender.menshealth3

Avery. (2018, September 7). Kino Escalation: How To Attract Women With Physical Touch -. Retrieved February 17, 2020, from https://redpilltheory.com/2018/09/06/kino-escalation-how-to-attract-women-with-physical-touch/

Barbe, O. (2004, November 5). Sex on the Brain. Retrieved February 18, 2020, from https://www.menshealth.com/sex-women/a19516672/understanding-sex-and-the-brain/

Barking Up the Wrong Tree. (n.d.). Seduction, Power and Mastery: 3 Lessons From History's Greatest Minds. Retrieved February 20, 2020, from https://www.bakadesuyo.com/2014/02/seduction-power-mastery/

BBC. (n.d.). Unpacking the Psychology of Seduction. Retrieved February 20, 2020, from https://www.bbc.com/reel/video/p07l3r3q/unpacking-the-psychology-of-seduction

Bergreen, L. (2017, July 26). 10 Seduction Tips and Tricks from Casanova Himself. Retrieved February 16, 2020, from https://www.tipsonlifeandlove.com/love-and-relationships/10-seduction-tips-and-tricks-from-casanova

Best PUA Training. (2018, May 3). Kino Escalation - Early, Mid Set Kino and Kiss Closing. Retrieved February 17, 2020, from http://www.bestpuatraining.com/kino-escalation

Bey, B. A. (2018, October 29). Here's Why Pitching is a Lot Like Seduction. Retrieved February 19, 2020, from https://www.mediabistro.com/climb-the-ladder/skills-expertise/heres-why-pitching-is-a-lot-like-seduction/

BigEyeUg3. (2017, June 6). 4 Signs you are too easily seduced. Retrieved February 10, 2020, from https://bigeye.ug/4-signs-you-are-too-easily-seduced/

Black Rose - Free Download PDF. (n.d.). Retrieved February 17, 2020, from https://kupdf.net/download/black-rose_58e52d47dc0d609438da97f1_pdf

Brandstory. (2016, September 3). The art of seduction – how to get customers to want you. Retrieved February 19, 2020, from http://www.brandstoryonline.com/seduction/

Britannica. (n.d.). Seduction. Retrieved February 15, 2020, from https://www.britannica.com/topic/seductio

Brizendine, L. (2010, March 25). Love, sex and the male brain - CNN.com. Retrieved February 18, 2020, from http://edition.cnn.com/2010/OPINION/03/23/brizendine.male.brain/index.html

Broucaret, F. (2014, December 23). Seduction: 10 Gestures and What They Reveal. Retrieved February 18, 2020, from https://www.mariefranceasia.com/lifelove/decoding/les-10-gestes-seduction-du-desir-59008.html#item=1

Buffalmano, L. (2019, November 2). How to Mind Fuck a Guy: The Ultimate Guide (With Examples). Retrieved February 18, 2020, from https://thepowermoves.com/make-him-crazy-about-you/

Burras, J. (n.d.). Power: Domination or Seduction. Retrieved February 18, 2020, from http://www.jonburras.com/pdfs/Power-Domination-or-Seduction.pdf

Calo, C. (n.d.). Switching From Logical to Social: The Art of Seduction. Retrieved February 7, 2020, from https://www.waytoosocial.com/the-art-of-seduction-blog/

Carter, G. L., Campbell, A., & Muncer, S. (2013, June 12). The Dark Triad Personality: Attractiveness to Women. Retrieved February 7, 2020, from https://scottbarrykaufman.com/wp-content/uploads/2013/09/The-Dark-Triad-Personality.pdf

Chamorro-Premuzic, T. (2015, November 4). Why Bad Guys Win at Work. Retrieved February 8, 2020, from https://hbr.org/2015/11/why-bad-guys-win-at-work

Coast, M. (2019a, November 4). 3 Ways to Trigger The Hero Instinct in Your Man. Retrieved February 18, 2020, from https://commitmentconnection.com/3-ways-to-trigger-the-hero-instinct-in-your-man/

Coast, M. (2019b, November 4). The Secret to Understanding What Triggers Emotional Attraction in Men. Retrieved February 18, 2020, from https://commitmentconnection.com/the-secret-to-understanding-what-triggers-attraction-in-men/

Cool Communicator. (2019, November 12). Social Seduction, Creating Space and Anticipation. Retrieved February 7, 2020, from https://coolcommunicator.com/social-seduction-creating-space-anticipation/

Cowie, A. (2017, May 22). The Enchanted Sex-Word of Scotland's Secret Seduction

Society. Retrieved February 8, 2020, from https://www.ancient-origins.net/history/enchanted-sex-word-scotland-s-secret-seduction-society-008114

Cross, E. (2020, January 15). Obsession Phrases Review: What Makes Him Truly Obsessed With You? Retrieved February 18, 2020, from https://www.lovemakingexperts.com/obsession-phrases-review/

Definitions.net. (n.d.). What Does Seduction Mean? Retrieved from https://www.definitions.net/definition/seduction

Dictionary.com. (n.d.). Seduce. Retrieved from https://www.dictionary.com/browse/seduce

Drapkin, J. (2005, May 1). Hpw to Seduce a Lover. Retrieved February 18, 2020, from https://www.psychologytoday.com/us/articles/200505/how-seduce-lover

Edwards, D. (n.d.). Seduction or abuse? Is seducing someone ethical or is it manipulation? Retrieved February 15, 2020, from https://steemit.com/ethics/@dana-edwards/seduction-or-abuse-is-seducing-someone-ethical-or-is-it-manipulation

Eliason, N. (n.d.). The Art of Seduction by Robert Greene: Summary, Notes, and Lessons. Retrieved February 15, 2020, from https://www.nateliason.com/notes/art-seduction-robert-greene

Emory University. (2004, March 16). Study Finds Male And Female Brains Respond Differently To Visual Stimuli. Retrieved February 18, 2020, from https://www.sciencedaily.com/releases/2004/03/040316072953.htm

Essays Writers. (n.d.). Persuasion, Manipulation and Seduction. Retrieved February 7, 2020, from https://essayswriters.com/essays/Analysis/persuasion-manipulation-and-seduction.html

Farouk Radwan, M. (n.d.). Why women like men with dark triad traits | 2KnowMySelf. Retrieved February 8, 2020, from https://www.2knowmyself.com/Why_women_like_men_with_dark_triad_traits

Farquhar, S. (2017, September 3). Shogun Method *. Retrieved February 17, 2020, from https://seductionfaq.com/blog/shogun-method/

Female Psychology. (n.d.). Retrieved February 17, 2020, from http://www.the-alpha-lounge.com/female-psychology.html

Finkelstein, K. (n.d.). The Influence of the Dark Triad and Gender on Sexual Coercion Strategies of a Subclinical Sample. Retrieved February 7, 2020, from https://bir.brandeis.edu/bitstream/handle/10192/28572/FinkelsteinThesis2014.pdf?sequence=1

Fisher, D. (n.d.). 7 Quick Tips to Help You Learn Seduction Faster | Girls Chase. Retrieved February 16, 2020, from https://www.girlschase.com/content/7-quick-tips-help-you-learn-seduction-faster

Francis, M. (2007, January 3). The psychology of seduction. Retrieved February 18, 2020, from https://www.dailymail.co.uk/femail/article-426320/The-psychology-seduction.html

Ganz, M. (2013, October 31). Covert Seduction – How to Mess with Women's Minds.

Retrieved February 17, 2020, from https://sibg.com/covert-seduction-mess-with-womens-minds/

Ganz, M. (2016, August 4). Black Rose Sequence – How You Can Seduce Women Using Mind Control Enslavement. Retrieved February 17, 2020, from https://sibg.com/black-rose-sequence-how-you-can-seduce-women-using-mind-control-enslavement/

Ganz, M. (2020, February 4). Fractionation Seduction Technique: All You Need To Know! Retrieved February 17, 2020, from https://sibg.com/using-fractionation-in-seduction/

Get the Guy. (2010, December 21). The Player: Why Men Long To Be Casanovas And How To Spot If He Is One – Men's Personalities Part 3. Retrieved February 16, 2020, from https://www.howtogettheguy.com/blog/player-mens-personalities-part-3/

Greene, R. (n.d.). The Art of Seduction. Retrieved February 8, 2020, from http://radio.shabanali.com/the-art-of-seduction-robert-greene

Hardy, J. (2020, January 30). The History of the Seduction Community. Retrieved February 8, 2020, from https://historycooperative.org/the-history-of-the-seduction-community/

Her Way. (2020, February 13). The Best Thing That Is Going To Happen To You This Year Is You. Retrieved February 18, 2020, from https://herway.net/relationship/3-simple-ways-to-unlock-the-hero-instinct-in-your-man/

His Secret Passion. (2019, March 30). Best 8 His Secret Obsession Phrases That Make A Man Fall In Love. Retrieved February 18, 2020, from https://hissecretpassion.com/secret-obsession-phrases/

Honan, D. (2019, January 30). James Bond's guide to seduction. Retrieved February 8, 2020, from https://bigthink.com/think-tank/james-bonds-guide-to-seduction

Hyman, R. (n.d.). Cold Reading: How to Convince Strangers That You Know All About Them. Retrieved February 17, 2020, from https://web.archive.org/web/20140716020736/http://www.skepdic.com/Hyman_cold_reading.htm

kartjoe. (2017, April 4). A modern man living guide to seduction PDF EBook Download-FREE. Retrieved February 7, 2020, from https://www.slideshare.net/kartjoe/a-modern-man-living-guide-to-seduction-pdf-ebook-downloadfree

Kaufman, S. (2015, December 10). The Myth of the Alpha Male. Retrieved February 8, 2020, from https://greatergood.berkeley.edu/article/item/the_myth_of_the_alpha_male

Kings of the Web. (2020, February 6). Cold Reading Is A Potent Seduction Tactic. Retrieved February 17, 2020, from https://heartiste.net/cold-reading-is-a-potent-seduction-tactic/

Kozmala, M. (2019, February 2). The Body language of seduction. Retrieved February 18, 2020, from https://businessandprestige.pl/the-body-language-of-seduction/

Lizra, C. (2017, December 10). Seduction in Business. Retrieved February 19, 2020, from https://www.powerofsomaticintelligence.com/blog/seduction-in-business

LoDolce, A. (2019, October 24). How to Seduce Men With Body Language: 12 Perfect Seduction Tips. Retrieved February 18, 2020, from https://sexyconfidence.com/how-to-seduce-men-with-body-language/

LoDolce, A. (2017, September 14). How To Scientifically Trigger His Emotional Desire for You using This Technique. Retrieved February 18, 2020, from https://www.huffpost.com/entry/how-to-scientifically-trigger-his-emotional-desire_b_59bab8b4e4b06b71800c3781

M., S. (2020, January 4). Shogun Method Review (Is Derek Rake The Real Deal?). Retrieved February 17, 2020, from https://www.calpont.com/shogun-method/

Madsen, P. (20212, July 7). The Power of Seduction. Retrieved February 7, 2020, from https://www.psychologytoday.com/us/blog/shameless-woman/201207/the-power-seduction

Magical Apparatus. (2019, December 1). The phases of a seduction - Alpha Male. Retrieved February 13, 2020, from https://www.magicalapparatus.com/alpha-male/the-phases-of-a-seduction.html

Magical Apparatus. (2019, December 26). Using Cold Reading - Seduction. Retrieved February 17, 2020, from https://www.magicalapparatus.com/seduction-2/chapter-ix-using-cold-reading.html

Mallens, T. (2015, September 4). 3 rules the art of seduction can teach you to boost your sales & marketing. Retrieved February 19, 2020, from https://www.linkedin.com/pulse/3-rules-art-seduction-can-teach-you-boost-your-sales-mallens-bsc-mba

Martin, C. (2010, November 11). Persuasion, Manipulation, Seduction, and Human Communication. Retrieved February 7, 2020, from http://opinionsandperspectives.blogspot.com/2010/11/persuasion-manipulation-seduction-and.html

Martin, T. (n.d.). Creating A More Effective B to B Sales Prospecting Program. Retrieved February 19, 2020, from https://conversedigital.com/social-selling-sales-training-posts/b-to-b-sales-prospecting

MensXP.com. (n.d.). MensXP.com - India's largest Online lifestyle magazine for Men. Offering tips & advice on relationships, fashion, office, health & grooming. Retrieved February 17, 2020, from https://www.mensxp.com/dating/seduction-science-/600-cold-reading-her-mind.html

Merriam-Webster. (n.d.). "Negging" Moves Beyond the Bar. Retrieved February 16, 2020, from https://www.merriam-webster.com/words-at-play/negging-pick-up-artist-meaning

Nguyen, V. (2013, August 17). 7 Life Lessons to Learn from Pickup Artists. Retrieved February 20, 2020, from https://www.selfstairway.com/pickup-artists/

Nicky Woolf. (n.d.). "Negging": the anatomy of a dating trend. Retrieved February 17, 2020, from https://www.newstatesman.com/blogs/voices/2012/05/negging-latest-dating-trend

Nixon, R. (2016, March 23). 10 Things Every Woman Should Know About a Man's

Brain. Retrieved February 18, 2020, from https://www.livescience.com/14422-10-facts-male-brains.html

Oesch, N., & Miklousic, I. (2012). The Dating Mind: Evolutionary Psychology and the Emerging Science of Human Courtship. *Evolutionary Psychology*, *10*(5), 147470491201000. https://doi.org/10.1177/147470491201000511

Presaud, R., & Bruggen, P. (2015, August 15). The Sexy Sons Theory of What Women Are Attracted to in Men. Retrieved February 15, 2020, from https://www.psychologytoday.com/intl/blog/slightly-blighty/201508/the-sexy-sons-theory-what-women-are-attracted-in-men

Rake, D. (n.d.). How to Hook Up With Beautiful Women - Using "Player" Seduction Tactics. Retrieved February 16, 2020, from https://ezinearticles.com/?How-to-Hook-Up-With-Beautiful-Women---Using-Player-Seduction-Tactics&id=2481207

Rake, D. (2020, January 17). Shogun Method - A Critical (Self) Review *. Retrieved February 17, 2020, from https://derekrake.com/blog/#Four-Steps-To-Eternal-Enslavement-8211-The-IRAE-Model

Rauthmann, J. (2014, April 1). Mate attraction in the Dark Triad: Narcissists are hot, Machiavellians and psychopaths not. Retrieved February 8, 2020, from https://www.sciencedirect.com/science/article/abs/pii/S0191886913006582

Razzputin. (n.d.). Knowing How to Use Kino Effectively on Women. Retrieved Winter 160, 2020, from https://www.waytoosocial.com/how-to-use-kino-effectively/

Riggio, R. (2016, February 10). 6 Seductive Body Language Channels. Retrieved February 18, 2020, from https://www.psychologytoday.com/intl/blog/cutting-edge-leadership/201602/6-seductive-body-language-channels

Roberts, M. (2016, August 4). Black Rose Sequence®. Retrieved February 17, 2020, from https://sonicseduction.net/black-rose-sequence/

Rogell, B. E. (2013, August 26). Seduction tactics to boost your career. Retrieved February 19, 2020, from https://www.news.com.au/finance/work/seduction-tactics-to-boost-your-career/news-story/6fce129b118a03dfde4b68c4169ababf

Rogell, E. (2013, August 22). Seduction Tactics For Your Career. Retrieved February 19, 2020, from https://sea.askmen.com/entertainment/216/topten/seduction-tactics-for-your-career

Rolstad, A. (n.d.). The "Hover and Disqualify" Pickup Technique | Girls Chase. Retrieved February 17, 2020, from https://www.girlschase.com/content/hover-and-disqualify-pickup-technique

S, P. (2017, April 5). Raj Persaud: The Psychology of Seduction at TEDX U. of Bristol (transcript). Retrieved February 20, 2020, from https://singjupost.com/raj-persaud-the-psychology-of-seduction-at-tedxuniversityofbristol-transcript/

Seltzer, L. (2013, September 17). The Paradox of Seduction. Retrieved February 7, 2020, from https://www.psychologytoday.com/us/blog/evolution-the-self/201309/the-paradox-seduction

Shogun Method Fractionation - Free Download PDF. (n.d.). Retrieved February 17, 2020, from https://kupdf.net/download/shogun-method-fractionation_5913cf2adc0d60bf4c959eb0_pdf

Sicinski, A. (2018, December 8). Breaking Down the Intoxicating Art of Romantic Seduction. Retrieved February 10, 2020, from https://blog.iqmatrix.com/art-seduction

Simon, C. (2012, February 16). Don't be Seduced! 6 Crucial Warning Signs. Retrieved February 10, 2020, from https://www.psychologytoday.com/us/blog/bringing-sex-focus/201202/dont-be-seduced-six-crucial-warning-signs

Sinn, J. (n.d.). 3 Ways to Use Cold Reading to Attract Women. Retrieved February 17, 2020, from https://ezinearticles.com/?3-Ways-to-Use-Cold-Reading-to-Attract-Women&id=6169379

Skills Converged Ltd. (n.d.). Skills Converged > Body Language of Seduction. Retrieved February 18, 2020, from https://www.skillsconverged.com/FreeTrainingMaterials/BodyLanguage/BodyLanguageofSeduction.aspx

Snowden, J. (2020, February 7). Shogun Method: My Confession (A Review). Retrieved February 17, 2020, from https://sibg.com/shogun-method/

T, S. (2015a, November 5). The Three Types Of Game Pickup Artists Use To Attract Women: Part 2. Retrieved February 13, 2020, from http://seductioncommunity.com/attraction/the-three-types-of-game-pickup-artists-use-to-attract-women-part-2/

T, S. (2015b, November 5). The Three Types Of Game To Attract Women: Part 1. Retrieved February 13, 2020, from http://seductioncommunity.com/attraction/the-three-types-of-game-to-attract-women-part-1/

Tan, J. (2020, January 10). Customer Seduction: How to make customers LOVE your brand... Retrieved February 19, 2020, from https://www.referralcandy.com/blog/customer-seduction-make-customers-love-brand-infographic/

TED Talks: The power of Seduction in our Everyday Lives. (2013, July 30). Retrieved February 19, 2020, from https://www.payscale.com/career-news/2013/07/ted-talks-the-power-of-seduction-in-our-everyday-lives

The Doctor. (2019, August 27). The ethics of Seduction. Retrieved February 15, 2020, from https://thedoctorsdiary.com/women/ethics-of-seduction/

The Natural Lifestyles. (2015, February 11). Why Learning Seduction Is Not Optional. Retrieved February 20, 2020, from https://www.youtube.com/watch?v=onqLFdYY5Rw

Vandeweert, W. (2015, July 22). Use Cold Reading to Pick Up Girls. Retrieved February 17, 2020, from https://willemvandeweert.wixsite.com/cold-reading/single-post/2015/06/08/USE-COLD-READING-TO-PICK-UP-GIRLS

Van Edwards, V. (n.d.). The Alpha Female: 9 Ways You Can Tell Who Is an Alpha Woman. Retrieved February 8, 2020, from https://www.scienceofpeople.com/alpha-female/

Way, H. (2020, February 13). The Best Thing That Is Going To Happen To You This Year Is You. Retrieved February 17, 2020, from https://herway.net/love/8-ways-men-use-fractionation-seduction-make-fall-love/

Weiss, R. (2015, June 20). What Turns Guys On? Understanding Sexual Desire. Retrieved February 18, 2020, from https://www.psychologytoday.com/us/blog/love-and-sex-in-the-digital-age/201506/what-turns-guys-understanding-male-sexual-desire

Wendell, R. (n.d.). Cold Reading Your Way to Great Conversations | Girls Chase. Retrieved February 17, 2020, from https://www.girlschase.com/content/cold-reading-your-way-great-conversations

Williams, S. (2012, March 14). Are You Easily Seduced? Retrieved February 10, 2020, from https://www.yourtango.com/experts/shay-your-date-diva-williams/are-you-easy-be-seduced

Wilson, B. M. (2011, October 23). The great seducers. Retrieved February 8, 2020, from https://www.independent.co.uk/life-style/love-sex/seduction/the-great-seducers-928178.html

Wilson, J. (n.d.). Social Psychology: The Seduction of Consumers. Retrieved February 7, 2020, from https://pdfs.semanticscholar.org/be16/b695b47eee8f82e5af8ac3da2589d76b2799.pdf

Woman Knows: 12 Tricks That Men Use to Seduce Women. (n.d.). Retrieved February 16, 2020, from http://www.womanknows.com/understanding-men/news/71/

Woman Knows: Playboys: Uncovering the Mystery. (n.d.). Retrieved February 16, 2020, from http://www.womanknows.com/understanding-men/news/316/

Yohn, D. L. (2016, March 9). To Win Customers, Stop Selling And Start Seducing. Retrieved February 19, 2020, from https://www.forbes.com/sites/deniselyohn/2016/03/09/to-win-customers-stop-selling-and-start-seducing/#443e2ed451c1

EXCLUSIVE GIFT

Hello! Thank you for purchasing this book. Here is your free gift. It's good and it's free!

This mini e-book will answer your questions about this rather controversial skill. It's controversial because it works!

Get ready to learn more about Conversational Hypnosis, simplified for easy and practical use.

Here are just a few of the many benefits of learning Conversational Hypnosis:

- Get your audience to warm up to you and be more open to your message
- Better sales tactics
- Create deeper connections with people
- Create positive change
- And more!

If you want to become a good hypnotic conversationalist, you better start learning the skill today and be a master tomorrow. All you have to do is access the secret download page below.

Open a browser window on your computer or smartphone and enter: <u>bonus.emorygreen.com</u>

You will be automatically directed to the download page.

Remember to influence the world with good intentions.

All the best,
Emory Green

Printed in Great Britain
by Amazon